SEEING PROPHECY
FULFILLED IN PALESTINE

BY

GEORGE T. B. DAVIS

Author of

"FULFILLED PROPHECIES THAT PROVE THE BIBLE"

"REBUILDING PALESTINE ACCORDING TO PROPHECY"

THE MILLION TESTAMENTS CAMPAIGNS

1505 Race Street, Philadelphia, Pa.

Copyright, 1937
by
The Million Testaments Campaigns

First Printing 25,000 copies, November 15, 1937

Printed in the United States of America

REBUILDING PALESTINE IN TROUBLOUS TIMES
Long ago, under Nehemiah, the Jews wrought with their swords by their sides. During the riots this colonist ran a tractor with his carbine within easy reach.

CONTENTS

CHAPTER		PAGE
I.	Going to Jerusalem	7
II.	The Greater Return from Exile	16
III.	Visiting Colonies in Palestine	31
IV.	The Romance of Tel Aviv	43
V.	Making Palestine an Airway Center	56
VI.	Jerusalem the Transformed	67
VII.	Who Owns Palestine?	79
VIII	The Nehemiah of Modern Palestine	92
IX.	The Partition of Palestine	103
X.	The Future of the Jews	119

Chapter I

GOING TO JERUSALEM

Again we were "going to Jerusalem."

It was a happy little group gathered in the second class compartment of the train en route from ancient Lydda to Jerusalem. One of the passengers was a Jew who had lived in Australia for more than a quarter of a century, and was returning to his boyhood home in Jerusalem to see his aged father. Another was a Welsh clergyman, well advanced in years, but still full of fervor for the spread of the Gospel. The other three occupants were Americans: one, an around-the-world woman tourist from Ohio, and my wife and I.

It was early morning, bright and clear. We were full of eager expectancy as the train threaded its way among the Judean hills, ever climbing higher and higher in its ascent to Jerusalem, 2500 feet above sea-level. One of the group remarked that it was his custom to begin the day with the Word of God and asked if it would be agreeable to all to have a chapter read aloud. They heartily assented. The chapter read was Romans 9. It was peculiarly appropriate, being filled with references to both Jews and Gentiles. All listened intently, including our Jewish fellow passenger.

Then for a time the Welsh minister entertained us all with interesting experiences of preaching the Gospel in foreign lands. Moment by moment his spirit, or *hwyl* as they say in Wales, was becoming more and more aroused. At last he could contain himself no longer and burst into an old Gospel melody. His clear, rich tones rang joyfully through the car. It was not long until we caught the infection. Soon we were singing heartily one Gospel hymn after another. We used no "soft pedals" on our voices, and the people in the other compartments may have thought that we were a group of Salvation Army enthusiasts!

Our singing, however, did not hinder our enjoying the scenery along the way. At one stop we were surprised to see a garden with lovely flowers alongside the station, doubtless the work of a beauty-loving station master. But what most interested us, as the train climbed upward, was the progress that had been made in transforming the Judean hills from barrenness to beauty. A number of the hills were beautifully terraced and were planted with growing grain.

I had not remembered seeing these terraces even two years ago.

Presently the Arab ticket collector appeared. We showed him our tickets and a copy of an Arabic New Testament. He was delighted to receive it. A second railway employee, seeing the Arabic Testament, eagerly besought us for another copy. Alas, it was the only one we had left. However, we took his name and address and sent him a copy after our arrival in Jerusalem. Earlier in the journey, our Jewish fellow passenger had gratefully received a New Testament. Strangely enough, the round-the-world tourist had been given one of the campaign New Testaments while she was traveling on an inter-island steamer in the Philippines.

Thus, with singing, and sightseeing, and spreading God's Word, we journeyed on to Jerusalem. As the train came to a standstill in the Jerusalem station there was a hurried scramble to unload passengers and baggage. We caught a glimpse of the aged father of our Jewish friend. What joy must have been theirs as they embraced each other after a separation of more than a quarter of a century!

After making the customary bargain with a taxi driver we were taken to the home of Mr. and Mrs. Ralph Fried, in the Street of the Prophets.

Two years ago we had had the privilege of staying with them, and once again we enjoyed sweet fellowship in their home during our stay in Jerusalem.

During our almost seven weeks' stay in Palestine we were again amazed at the marvelous changes that have taken place during the past few years since the Jews have been returning to the land in such large numbers. Jerusalem, Tel Aviv, and Haifa are great flourishing modern cities. Swamp lands have been transformed into fertile fields. Sand dunes have given place to beautiful orange groves. The great plain of Esdraelon is dotted over with flourishing Jewish colonies. The plain of Sharon is once more like "a garden of Eden." The land that lay largely waste and desolate during the long centuries of the Jewish dispersion is again beginning to "blossom as the rose."

All this modern development of Palestine is the growing fulfillment of the predictions of the Old Testament prophets. A graphic picture of the changes that are taking place today was given more than 2500 years ago by the prophet Amos: "And I will bring again the captivity of my people of Israel, and they shall build the waste cities, and inhabit them; and they shall plant vineyards, and drink the wine thereof; they

JERUSALEM GROWS SOUTHWARD

Long ago the prophet Jeremiah predicted certain of Jerusalem's boundary lines, but no limit was placed on the growth of the city southward toward Bethlehem.

shall also make gardens, and eat the fruit of them. And I will plant them upon their land, and they shall no more be pulled up out of their land which I have given them, saith the Lord thy God" (Amos 9: 14, 15).

Truly the Lord is bringing again the captivity of the Jews who have been scattered to the ends of the earth for long centuries. They are indeed building "the waste cities," and planting "vineyards," and making "gardens." Further, the returning colonists are planting their roots deeply into "their land." And it is comforting to read the prophet's words that "they shall no more be pulled up out of their land which I have given them."

While in Palestine, we learned more fully than ever of the passionate love of the Jews for the land of their forefathers, and the longing to return to it that has burned in the breasts of orthodox Jews throughout the years of their long dispersion. We were told it is a common practice for devout Jews all over the world to rise at midnight, or in the early morning hours, to weep because of the destruction of Zion and to pray for its redemption.

Many Jews, even those who are very poor, will save their hard earned money to purchase a small bag of soil from Palestine that it may be laid

TEACHING JEWISH CHILDREN THE HEBREW ALPHABET
A German doctor in Palestine teaching young children the Hebrew alphabet by means of pictures.

under their head in their coffin. They feel that at least in death they are again united to the land of Palestine. It may be there is in this the hope that being joined to the land they will be raised again when the Messiah comes to Zion.

"Next year in Jerusalem" has been the heart-cry of the Jews, especially at Passover time, throughout the long period of their dispersion. More than once during the centuries definite plans have been made for their return. In the early days of America's history, the idea of a Jewish national home in Palestine found sympathetic support. John Adams, the second president of the United States, wrote a letter to Major Noah, a prominent American Jew, heartily commending the project. In Great Britain, Dean Stanley wrote: "The Jewish race, so wonderfully preserved, may yet have another stage of national existence opened to them. They may once more obtain possession of their native land."

The foremost exponent in the British Isles of the establishment of a Jewish home in Palestine was the seventh Earl of Shaftesbury. In 1838 he pleaded with various nations to co-operate in the project, saying: "Everything seems ripe for their return."

"Man proposes, but God disposes." The project was not accomplished. In the timepiece of God's eternal purposes the hour for the return of the Jews had not yet struck. It was only after the World War that the words of the psalmist were fulfilled: "Thou shalt arise, and have mercy upon Zion: for the time to favor her, yea, the set time, is come" (Psalm 102: 13).

This is indeed "the set time" to favor Zion. All the world is witnessing the way in which the God of Israel is helping forward and is directing the work of rebuilding Palestine even in troublous times. No one will deny that the Jews have worked hard and heroically. But the remarkable results that have been achieved are due first and foremost to the favor and blessing of God upon their efforts. The transformation that has taken place in Palestine during the past fifteen years is perhaps unparalleled in history in so short a space of time.

In the succeeding chapters we hope to tell of the continued growth of the colonies and of the cities, such as Tel Aviv and Jerusalem; of the tragic loss of life and destruction of property during the strike and riots of 1936; of the new crises that are confronting both Jews and Arabs through the suggested partition of the land; and to answer from God's Word the question, "Who owns Palestine?" and to tell of the future glory of the land and of the chosen people.

Chapter II

THE GREATER RETURN FROM EXILE

The second and far greater return of the Jews from exile is taking place in Palestine today before our eyes. It is one of the most interesting and amazing spectacles of modern times.

And the remarkable thing about this present-day migration to Palestine is that it so precisely parallels the previous return more than 2500 years ago. At that time, under the leadership of Ezra and Nehemiah, some 42,000 Jews returned from Babylon to rebuild Jerusalem. Today many times that number have returned from exile, not from one land, but from many lands. And they have gone back not simply to rebuild Jerusalem, but to transform the land of Palestine.

The similarity between the two returns is so striking that it cannot be a mere coincidence. It is nothing less than the guiding hand of the God of Abraham, Isaac, and Jacob directing this greater modern return even as He did the previous one long ago.

Let us look at some of the remarkable parallels between the two returns. The first striking analogy is found in the fact that the Jews went back from Babylon to Jerusalem with the consent and encouragement of Cyrus, King of Persia, the ruler of the greatest empire of that day. In our day they have been returning to Palestine with the permission, and under the protection of Great Britain, the greatest empire of our generation.

Another significant fact is that when the Jews went back under Ezra and Nehemiah they found Jerusalem in ruins, and their first task was that of rebuilding. So in our day the returning Jews have found the whole land largely waste and desolate, and once again they are laboring with might and main at the task of reconstruction.

A third exact parallel between the two returns is that the work of rebuilding has in each case been violently opposed by those living in the land when the Jews returned to the heritage of their forefathers. During the period of 70 years that the Jews were in captivity in Babylon, other races had settled on the land. They strongly resented the reappearance of the exiles, and did all in their power to prevent the rebuilding of the Temple and the wall of Jerusalem.

The books of Ezra and Nehemiah abound in graphic descriptions of the efforts of those occupying the country to thwart the task of rebuilding. In Ezra 4: 4 we read: "Then the people of the land weakened the hands of the people of Judah, and troubled them in building." Could any phrase describe more accurately the efforts of the Arabs of our day to harass the Jews in their work of rehabilitating Palestine?

Ezra further tells how the foes of the Jews not only made repeated efforts to hinder the work locally, but even went so far as to appeal to the Persian government to stop the rebuilding. They sent a strong letter of complaint to Artaxerxes, a later ruler of the Persian realm, telling what a calamity it would be to have Jerusalem rebuilt! Curiously enough their complaint succeeded, and Artaxerxes sent back word that the work must be stopped at once. Ezra records the temporary stoppage of the task: "Then ceased the work of the house of God which is at Jerusalem. So it ceased unto the second year of the reign of Darius King of Persia" (Ezra 4: 24).

How the Palestine Arabs of today are following in the footsteps of their predecessors of long ago! They, too, have been using the double method of harassing the Jews locally, and of making repeated appeals to the British Government to stop immigration, and so cause the work of reconstruction to cease.

But in the days of Ezra and Nehemiah the work of rebuilding was soon recommenced with redoubled vigor. In Ezra 5: 5 we are told that "the eye of their God was upon the elders of the Jews, that they [their enemies] could not cause them to cease." The people of the land were astonished at the rapid progress the returned Jews were making in the work of rebuilding. They sent a letter to King Darius in which they said: "This work goeth fast on, and prospereth in their hands" (Ezra 5: 8). This same statement could well be used to picture the progress made in rebuilding Palestine in the present generation.

In the olden days, as in our time, the success of the work of rebuilding Palestine stirred the foes of the Jews to still greater antagonism. First they mocked the Jews. When they saw this did not avail they determined to fight against them. Their angry opposition is recorded in Nehemiah 4: 7, 8: "Then they were very wroth, and conspired all of them together to come and to fight against Jerusalem, and to hinder it."

So during the past fifteen or twenty years as the Arabs have witnessed the Jews returning in ever increasing numbers, and have seen the land being transformed from barrenness to beauty, and the waste cities being rebuilt, their opposition has steadily increased. There were violent outbursts against the Jews in 1920, 1921, and 1929. But the riots of 1936 were the climax of all the

Arab efforts to stop further immigration of the Jews into Palestine.

The first move of the Arab leaders was to organize a nation-wide strike to show the British government that they were willing to make any sacrifice to stop the stream of Jews pouring into Palestine. This plan did not succeed. Then they started rioting, and the strike and riots continued for a period of six months. Hundreds of thousands of carefully planted trees were detroyed, crops were burned, business was crippled, houses were demolished, trains were wrecked, a reign of terror was inaugurated, and a hundred Jews were slain. The British poured troops into Palestine, but it was only when martial law was finally proclaimed, and neighboring Arab rulers appealed for peace, that the riots ceased.

During our stay in Palestine I secured an eye-witness account of the strike and riots from one who was in the country during the entire time of the trouble. My informant loves both the Jews and the Arabs, and was greatly grieved that the Arabs should have resorted to such excesses to achieve their object. He said:

"The trouble began at Jaffa, which is a purely Arab town. A score or more of Jews were killed during the first day or two of the riots. The third day the disturbances reached Jerusalem. They

GUARDING THE WORKERS DURING THE RIOTS

The task of rebuilding Palestine went right on during the riots, but laborers went to their work guarded by the guns of extra policemen.

broke out in the old city and spread to the new Jewish quarter. One night three shots were fired from the darkness into a Jewish crowd coming out of a movie theatre. Three Jews were killed outright.

"A few days later the Arabs presented to the Palestine government three demands as follows:

"First, a complete stoppage of Jewish immigration.

"Second, an edict forbidding the sale of land to the Jews.

"Third, the establishment of a national (Arab) government.

"The Palestine government refused to take any action or even consider the three demands until violence was stopped. A few days later the Arab Higher Committee, of which the Grand Mufti is the president, called for a general strike throughout Palestine, and the boycotting of the Jews both commercially and socially.

"The strike of the Arabs was fully carried out in most parts of Palestine and lasted for six months. The situation in Jerusalem during the strike was typical of what took place throughout the country. All Arab stores and workshops were closed, but the Arab newspapers were allowed to appear daily. All Arab buses and taxis stopped running.

"The Arabs did everything in their power to prevent the running of Jewish and government cars. Large tacks, about one and a half inches long, were thickly strewn on the streets of Jerusalem to paralyze traffic. One taxi firm with twenty cars had one hundred and fifty punctures in one day. Some Jewish cars tied brooms in front of the wheels to sweep away the tacks, and police went to and fro sweeping them up in great piles.

"When the Arabs saw that the strike did not accomplish their purpose, they began using violence. Bands of armed Arabs roamed Palestine. Each Arab village was compelled by the strike committee to furnish its quota of money or men. Travel on the highways became very dangerous. Almost daily there were hold-ups and killings. Bands of Arabs went from place to place at night, rooting up orange trees and grape vines and burning fields of grain.

"At length they became still bolder. They began attacking the railway line, loosening rails, and blowing up small bridges. As a result several trains were wrecked. For months the passenger trains were heavily guarded with soldiers at each window with rifles ready for action. A special military car went in front of the train, and an airplane flew overhead. But trains were fired on continually.

"About two weeks after the strike began, curfew was declared in Jerusalem and in other cities. No one was permitted on the streets after 7 P. M. Each night Arab bands from the villages would come up to the outskirts of Jerusalem and would fire shots for hours to terrorize the people of the city. Armed trucks of British soldiers would go out to scatter the bands.

"For a time, Jewish bus traffic between Jerusalem and Tel Aviv continued regularly every fifteen minutes. But soon that had to be abandoned. Volleys of bullets were fired at them from hiding places along the road. Later, only four buses ran daily, and these were convoyed with military trucks, fitted with machine guns, going before and behind the buses.

"Before the trouble began, the native Jews and Arabs had lived together in harmony in the old city of Jerusalem. These native Jews spoke Arabic and dressed like Arabs and their shops and homes were intermingled. However, after the riots began, the incited hatred of the Arabs against the Jews became so intense that they began to kill some of them and to loot their shops. One of the most pathetic sights we witnessed during the riots was to see Jews fleeing for their

A WRECKED RAILWAY TRAIN IN PALESTINE
This train was wrecked by the Arabs during the riots of 1936.

HOUSES WRECKED DURING THE RIOTS
Jewish homes, on the outskirts of Tel Aviv, destroyed by Arabs during the rioting.

lives out of the old city, with a baby and a bundle of clothing, to find shelter in a more protected Jewish quarter outside the walls of old Jerusalem. In the newer parts of the city also, the Arab and Jewish quarters became like enemies' camps—no Jew daring to go into the Arab section, and no Arab venturing into the Jewish quarter.

"British troops by the thousands began pouring into Palestine. However, in spite of the presence of the large number of troops, violence and terror increased continually. Heavy fines were imposed on villages that concealed bands of marauders, and many Arab strike leaders were sent to concentration camps in the desert south of Beersheba.

"The aim of the strike was to show the British Government how desperate the Arabs were over the large influx of Jews into Palestine. With one voice they insisted that they would never give up until the government granted their demand—that Jewish immigration be entirely stopped. Finally, however, after six months of terror, both the strike and the violence were called off at the request of the Arab rulers of neighboring countries.

"The British did not yield to the Arab demand that Jewish immigration be suspended, but after the strike it was greatly curtailed. Later, a Royal

JEWISH IMMIGRATION MUST BE STOPPED!
Arabs vowing to do all in their power to stop the further influx of Jews into Palestine.

Commission was sent by the British Government to study the underlying causes of the trouble and to suggest a solution. At first the Arabs refused to testify before the commission, but later did so and added a fourth demand—the abrogation of both the Balfour Declaration and the British Mandate over Palestine."

The riots by no means succeeded in stopping the task of rebuilding Palestine. The work went forward in spite of all the furious opposition of the Arabs. The life-drama of Nehemiah's time was re-enacted in 1936 with intense reality. Nehemiah tells us how they prayed and then took further courageous action: "Nevertheless we made our prayer unto our God, and set a watch against them day and night, because of them."

Precisely the same procedure was followed during the 1936 riots. Three times the rabbis called for a day of fasting and prayer, and we were informed that the days were quite generally observed throughout the land. And they "set a watch" against their foes just as Nehemiah had done long ago. Signallers were stationed at strategic points. They flashed news of disturbances from one end of the land to the other. Watchmen were also appointed in various colonies to notify the settlers of the approach of marauding Arabs.

One of the most remarkable of all the parallels is that the same methods of defense were adopted for the 1936 riots as had been used by Nehemiah long ago. He describes his program of protection in chapter 4, verses 17 and 18: "They which builded on the wall, and they that bare burdens, with those that laded, every one with one of his hands wrought in the work, and with the other hand held a weapon. For the builders, every one had his sword girded by his side, and so builded."

The very same plan of rebuilding Palestine with weapons at hand was followed during the riots. The Jewish colonies were unprotected, as the British troops were stationed in the cities. The government therefore issued a thousand rifles to certain colonists and appointed them supernumerary police. As the riots grew in intensity further supplies of rifles were sent out until the number reached four thousand. Thus the colonists went about their work with their weapons at hand exactly as was the case long ago—only the modern arm of defense was a rifle instead of a sword. Could one conceive of a more complete similarity between two events—and yet they were separated by a period of 2500 years!

While in Jerusalem it was our privilege to have another interview with the young man at the Jewish Agency who had given us such helpful information two years before. He told us that the fourth chapter of Nehemiah had been a great comfort and help to the people of Palestine during the riots. He said a Jewish composer living in one of the colonies had set the chapter to music and that it was sung throughout the land.

It is little short of miraculous, and reveals the overruling providence of God, that the troublous times of the riots should have been such an exact repetition of those of long ago. But there is one event of the days of Ezra and Nehemiah that still lacks its modern counterpart. It is recorded in Nehemiah 6:15 in one brief sentence: "So the wall was finished in the twenty and fifth day of the month Elul, in fifty and two days." The task was not left incomplete. It was successfully finished! And another very significant phrase occurs at the end of the next verse: "They perceived that this work was wrought of our God."

So in full confidence we may rest assured that the far greater work of rebuilding Palestine will be completed in due course in spite of all past, present, and future opposition. We may also be sure that when it is finished not only the Arabs, but all other peoples of the earth as well, will see that the task of transforming the land was "wrought of our God." Truly "this is the Lord's doing; it is marvelous in our eyes."

Chapter III

VISITING COLONIES IN PALESTINE

More than two hundred Jewish colonies have planted their roots deeply in the soil of Palestine during the past fifty years. The establishment and development of these colonies in the face of great difficulties is one of the most heroic achievements in the rebuilding of Palestine.

Jewish settlers have come from all parts of the world to work with courage and fortitude in helping to transform the land from a wilderness to a country of fruitful fields and flourishing vineyards. The colonists realize that they are laboring not simply to earn a living but to have a real and vital share in the redemption of the land.

The task of the settlers who have returned to Palestine has not been an easy one. For centuries, during the long dispersion of the Jews, the land lay largely waste and desolate. The people who had lived in the country for generations had done little or nothing to improve the soil, so gradually it had become barren and unfruitful. For example, the once fertile and populous plain of Esdraelon, which was a part of ancient Galilee, had largely degenerated into a swamp land infested with malaria.

An eyewitness gives the following pen picture of the plain of Esdraelon as it appeared before the Jews began to return in large numbers to Palestine: "When I first saw it in 1920 it was a desolation. Four or five small squalid Arab villages, long distances from one another, could be seen on the summits of low hills here and there. For the rest, the country was uninhabited. There was not a house, not a tree. Along the branch of the Hedjaz Railway an occasional train stopped at deserted stations. A great part of the soil was in the ownership of absentee Syrian landlords. The River Kishon which flows through the valley, and the many springs that feed it from the hillsides, had been allowed to form a series of swamps and marshes. As a consequence, the country was infested with malaria. Besides, public security had been so bad under the former régime, that any settled agriculture was almost impossible."

Today the plain of Esdraelon is dotted over with flourishing Jewish colonies. As we drove along the Megiddo road and looked out over the vast valley filled with fields of waving grain, it formed one of the most pleasing pictures of our recent visit to Palestine.

The neighboring plain of Sharon has also

FAIR HELPERS IN THE FIELDS OF PALESTINE
Pioneer Jewish girls helping to transform the land from barrenness to beauty.

A JOY RIDE ON A PALESTINE DONKEY
Donkeys in Palestine are used to bearing heavy burdens, so this one does not seem troubled by his triple load.

undergone a remarkable transformation during the past twenty years. Our souls were thrilled by the story of the founding and development of one of the oldest settlements in the plain, that of the Hadera colony. A friend in Jerusalem gave us a booklet he had written containing a stirring account of some of the struggles of the early settlers of this colony.

Hadera was established in a district "notorious for its deadly swamps. No railway was available. The roads were bad and dangerous. Neighboring bedouins prowled about the huts, stealing whatever they could. Soon malaria broke out among the settlers. One after another of the pioneers was felled, old men, little children, and young laborers. The settlers could not afford a resident physician, and the nearest hospital was many hours away."

The situation became desperate. The question arose as to whether the settlement should be abandoned. One of the colonists in Hadera has written an account of how the crisis was faced with heroic fortitude: "Things went from bad to worse. The mark of death was on our foreheads, the certainty of death in our hearts. Friends and relatives came from other parts of Palestine, pleading with us to leave. 'Save your lives!' they begged. 'Save the good name of Palestine!'

Nevertheless, no man stirred from his place. Were we to run away from the battle? Leave Hadera to revert to its former state? How could we? Some even said: 'Better to die for Hadera than to live without her!' "

The colony lost almost all of its early settlers. They fought heroically against malaria, but it was years before it was finally overcome. In spite of all their trials they went steadily forward with the work of redeeming the soil. Was their sacrifice worth while? The answer is given in this description of the colony as it is at the present time: "Today, Hadera is one of the most flourishing agricultural colonies. It has some 5000 settlers, and more than 700 houses. Malaria has been completely stamped out. Great orchards of oranges and grapefruit, lemons and citron, surround the colony, which recently has become a center of meat and dairy produce."

Since those early days of the founding of Hadera, great advances have been made in colonization methods in Palestine. Larger funds, also, have been made available to help the settlers in scientifically combating malaria and other pioneer difficulties. This progress made in colonization work in Palestine would scarcely have been possible save through the wise guidance and financial co-operation of the Jewish Agency and its allied organizations. Through these combined channels more than fifty million dollars have been subscribed by Jews throughout the world for what might be called non-commercial colonization work in Palestine,—such as draining swamps, land improvements, agricultural and industrial experiments, and health and educational services.

The Jewish colonies are conducted along the lines of the latest scientific methods of agriculture. They specialize in intensive cultivation in order to secure the largest yield from each acre of soil. The colonizing work in Palestine has been greatly helped forward by the Agricultural Experiment Station at Rehovoth and its several branches. They constantly send out literature to the settlements giving the latest results of their experiments. This has greatly increased the efficiency of the colonies.

After spending some time in Jerusalem we were eager to revisit Rehovoth where we had had such an enjoyable time two years before. One morning we left the city in a motor car, accompanied by our good friends, Mr. Raad, the well-known Jerusalem photographer, and Mr. Shacknai, the secretary of the Zionist Information Bureau in Jerusalem.

On our arrival at the Research Headquarters

"Sonny" Among the Peaches
The little son of a Jewish colonist in the midst of a Palestine peach tree.

Grandparents and Little Ones at Home
Many elderly Jews are coming to Palestine to spend their last days in the country for which they yearned.

we received a cordial welcome. The secretary of the station was again most kind in giving us information about the progress that is being made along agricultural lines. One of the things that most interested us was a model farm of five acres. The project is being carried on to demonstrate the fact that five acres of land in Palestine will provide a good living for a family of five. The farm is being conducted on the most scientific lines. Careful records are being kept and the experiment is working successfully.

Together with the secretary of the station we inspected the neat little cottage occupied by the farmer and his household. In the living room the elderly grandfather had been reading and becoming weary had thrown a mantle about him and fallen asleep on the couch before our coming. On the center table was the open book he had been reading when his eyes had grown heavy. It was the book of Psalms in large type with comments or explanations by venerated rabbis. It gave us a thrill of pleasure to come into this colonists' home on a surprise visit and find there those who realize that "man doth not live by bread only, but by every word that proceedeth out of the mouth of the Lord."

Presently the farmer came in from the fields and Mr. Raad took a picture of him, and of a fellow workman from the station, as they stood near the little farmhouse. Before leaving, we presented them both with copies of the New Testament in Hebrew. They readily accepted the attractive little books and seemed to appreciate them.

Leaving the experiment station we motored some fifty miles northward to the Nathaniah colony. We had heard that the High Commissioner for Palestine, Sir Arthur Wauchope, was to be there that day to plant an olive tree on behalf of King George VI. The journey was both interesting and enjoyable. We passed through Rishon le Zion, one of the best known colonies in Palestine. Large vineyards abound in the district. The colony produces both wine and unfermented grapejuice. Mile after mile, as we continued our journey, we motored through districts planted with beautiful orange groves. What a transformation from the barren sand dunes of a few years ago to the fruitful orange groves of today!

Later we passed through Petah-Tikva, one of the oldest and largest of all the settlements in Palestine. It has a population of 16,000 and has recently been made a municipality. Soon we came to the new coastal highway that is being built to connect Tel Aviv with Haifa. Before the 1936 riots, it was a rough country road. Today it is a smooth asphalt highway, through a district dotted with Jewish colonies.

Arriving at Nathaniah, we enjoyed a well cooked chicken dinner at a hotel in the colony, and then went with hundreds of others to see the ceremony. The tree planting by the High Commissioner was an interesting experience. Sir Arthur walked to the appointed place through two lines of colonists' children, many of them wearing the colorful blue which is such a favorite among the Zionists. We stood on a little knoll watching the proceedings. After the ceremony the High Commissioner made a brief address telling of his interest in the land and in the colonies.

That afternoon we motored southward to Tel Aviv along the famous plain of Sharon. It was suggested that we stop at a near-by settlement where they specialize in poultry farming. This colony is quite unique in the fact that a large proportion of the colonists there had been professional men—including seventeen doctors, eight lawyers, and a university lecturer! We had a pleasant chat with a stalwart colonist who had spent several years in consular service in New York City. As he told us of the work of the colony we realized that they were throwing them-

AN ANCIENT WELL AT BEERSHEBA
Deep wells of 500 and 600 feet are being bored to find water. They are in striking contrast to this ancient well.

A HOME ON THE MODEL FARM
Experiments are being made in Palestine to show that five acres of land will provide support for five persons.

selves into the business of raising poultry with the same zeal and enthusiasm that they had doubtless displayed in their former practice as doctors and lawyers.

Fifty families in this colony have poultry farms, and each family has at least 600 fowls. They specialize in white leghorns. We saw some of the poultry runs, or enclosures, and the beautiful white fowls made a pleasing picture. The annual sale of eggs by the members of the colony reaches a total of two and a half million!

But what most interested and surprised us was their hatches of young chicks. They have two electric incubators—made in America—with a combined capacity of 36,000 eggs at one loading! When I asked what percentage of the eggs hatched out, we were told it was about 70 to 75 per cent. Think of it, having a family of 25,000 little "fuzzies" on their hands at one time!

That evening we arrived in Tel Aviv, tired but happy after a full day of sight-seeing. We had visited various colonies and had witnessed the marvelous transformation that is taking place in the land since the Jews have been returning to their ancient heritage. All we saw was abundant confirmation of the restoration of Palestine predicted by the Old Testaments prophets 2500 years ago!

Chapter IV

THE ROMANCE OF TEL AVIV

Tel Aviv is one of the most interesting and remarkable cities in the world today. The story of its founding and rapid growth reads more like fiction than actual fact.

Thirty years ago the land on which the city stands was scarcely more than a series of sand dunes on the shore of the Mediterranean Sea. Today Tel Aviv is the metropolis of Palestine, with a population of 150,000 people, and still growing rapidly.

Tel Aviv is unique in that it is probably the only all-Jewish city in the world. From beginning to end everything in the city is Jewish. The newspapers are printed in the Hebrew language; the conversation on the streets and in the homes is chiefly in Hebrew; the teaching in the schools is in the Hebrew tongue; the streets are named largely after Hebrew people; the shop signs are in Hebrew; the policemen are Hebrews—in short, it is a Jewish city from center to circumference.

When we revisited Tel Aviv, after a period of two years, we were again impressed with the entire absence of the usual greetings of "Good Morning" and "Good Evening" that are so familiar in other cities throughout the world. Instead one hears on every side the beautiful and revived salutation of Biblical days. In the homes, on the streets, in the shops, everywhere, the greeting is *"Shalom"* (Peace), and the answer comes back *"Shalom."*

Tel Aviv is beautifully situated. It is not only on the shore of the Mediterranean, but also in the heart of the orange district. The city was doubtless called Tel Aviv after Tel Abib, where the Hebrew captives dwelt in the land of Chaldea by the river of Chebar. It is mentioned in Ezekiel 3:15. The name means "a mound of green growth," and modern Tel Aviv may well be termed "a garden city." One of the Rothschilds declared that Tel Aviv was "the springtime of the Hebrew nation after many hundreds of years of winter."

Following their long dispersion, the Lord is once more bringing the Jews back to their ancient heritage, and is blessing in no uncertain manner their task of rebuilding and repeopling the land. And Tel Aviv is one of the most outstanding examples of this work of transformation. Think of the sheer marvel of it—taking a sandy stretch of soil and building the metropolis of Palestine

FULFILLED IN PALESTINE 45

on it in less than thirty years! It is surely a fulfillment of the comforting prediction of Ezekiel in chapter thirty-six, verse eleven: "I will settle you after your old estates, and will do better unto you than at your beginnings."

We reached Tel Aviv late one afternoon after a busy day spent in visiting colonies. Arrangements had been made for us to spend the night at a small hotel near the sea. Quite in accordance with the character of the city the food was strictly "kosher." The lady in charge asked if we would like to have a "dairy dinner" as no milk could be served with meat. We assented, and enjoyed the delicious fresh fish, and vegetables and milk. Our room faced the sea, and from the front windows we had a beautiful view of the Mediterranean. Later we were lulled to sleep by the soft swish of the waves lapping the shore.

A Jewish friend in Jerusalem had kindly arranged for us to have an interview with Mr. Jehudah Nedivi, the Town Clerk of Tel Aviv. At the appointed hour the next morning we arrived at the City Hall. We were at once ushered into Mr. Nedivi's private office. Now the Town Clerk of a growing city like Tel Aviv is an exceedingly busy man. To our surprise Mr. Nedivi put aside his work and received us as cordially as though he had nothing in the world to do but to welcome visitors.

It was a warm summer morning and when we were seated Mr. Nedivi graciously asked what we would have to drink—orange juice or grapefruit juice. We suggested the latter as we had already enjoyed a generous supply of orange juice that morning. The interview lasted almost or quite an hour and proved to be one of the most delightful experiences of our stay in Palestine.

We learned that Mr. Nedivi came to Tel Aviv with his mother when he was a lad only fourteen years of age. At that time the town had only a few hundred inhabitants. Hence he has been an eyewitness of the growth of Tel Aviv from its early infancy. And in later years, in his capacity as Town Clerk, he has had no small share in the development of the city.

In response to his kind query as to what he could do for us, we told Mr. Nedivi that we were eager to hear the story of how Tel Aviv was started, and of its remarkable growth from a little town to a large, flourishing city. He replied that he would willingly lay asides statistics, and tell us the story.

Mr. Nedivi gave the narrative in beautiful English, although Hebrew was the language of

A BUSINESS CORNER IN TEL AVIV
Buses and motor cars abound in this throbbing city by the sea, where "Shalom" is the greeting of the people.

A VIEW OF TEL AVIV FROM THE SEA
The Jewish city of Tel Aviv is on the seashore, just north of the old Arab city of Jaffa.

his daily life. He had, however, scarcely begun the story when a voice in Hebrew came out of a little box on his desk. Without moving, just as he sat back in his chair, he answered in Hebrew. Presently the same thing was repeated. In response to my question as to what new thing this was, Mr. Nedivi explained that it was a radio telephone. It was rather remarkable that we had to go to far-off Palestine to witness something that we had never seen in our own land.

Then Mr. Nedivi launched into the story: "Tel Aviv was started as a residential and academic suburb of Jaffa. Jews who were in business in Jaffa wanted a place where they could live together quietly and educate their children. Some sixty heads of families settled here in 1908. Simultaneously with their coming they built a school, so education has been a vital factor in the life of the city from its very beginning.

"In those early days the town was under Turkish rule and its growth was not at all rapid. Six years later, when the World War began, the population of Tel Aviv was only about two thousand. During the war the suburb suffered severely. It was closed by the Turks, and the inhabitants, including our family, had to flee and find refuge elsewhere. Though we had to leave our homes and the school building, yet the classes of the school continued. They were held in the open air, and, along with others, I graduated under the trees in northern Palestine.

"At the conclusion of the war, and the beginning of the British occupation of Palestine, we returned to Tel Aviv. To our delight we found our homes and the school intact and in good condition. Several young men had courageously remained in the town, and had looked after the buildings while we were away.

"But the end of the war did not end our troubles. In 1921 intense Arab riots broke out and 42 Jews were killed in Jaffa. The Jewish people now realized that their lives were no longer safe in Jaffa where the population was overwhelmingly Arab. Hence the riots acted as a fresh stimulus to spur onward the growth of Tel Aviv.

"By the end of 1925 Tel Aviv was in the height of prosperity. It had reached a population of 35,000. Then came the financial crisis in many lands, and its severe repercussions reached us in Tel Aviv. But the depression was bravely met by a spirit of brotherly helpfulness on the part of the people. Many of those who were employed labored only three days a week in order to permit others to work the remaining three days. Others generously shared their wages with those in need.

At the same time the municipality did all in its power to create work for the unemployed.

"We successfully weathered the financial storm, but once again our troubles were not over. The passing of the depression was followed by fresh Arab riots in 1929. A cordon of guards was thrown around Tel Aviv with the result that only six lives were lost. Once more the riots served only to increase the growth and prosperity of the city. New people flocked into Tel Aviv, and new industries were started. The period from 1933 to 1935 was a time of unparalleled prosperity, and the city attained a population of 125,000."

Mr. Nedivi then came to the riots of 1936. He told of the heroism of the lorry drivers as they brought supplies of food to Tel Aviv during the time of the strike and rioting. Frequently the truck drivers were shot down as they drove their lorries along the roads leading to Tel Aviv, but others would at once take their places. He described the signaling that was carried on throughout the land during the disturbances, and said some of the most expert signaling work was done by boys and girls of school age. A girl who was signaling was shot. When the news reached Tel Aviv a. fourteen-year-old girl said to her mother, "Mummy, do you think I could take her place?"

ROTHSCHILD BOULEVARD IN TEL AVIV

This broad boulevard in the all-Jewish city reveals the remarkable achievement of transforming sand dunes into a great metropolis in thirty years.

Mr. Nedivi said: "The riots served only to plant the roots of the people and the city more deeply into the soil of Palestine. We were a community of Jews gathered from all parts of the world. We were free men and women living in the land of our forefathers, and we were determined to face the issues whatever they might be."

The riots proved to be a blessing in disguise to Tel Aviv, for they led to the building of a lighter port for the unloading of freight. Mr. Nedivi told with enthusiasm how Tel Aviv came to have its own port: "The port of Jaffa, near by, was closed by the strikers. The port of Haifa, up north, was choked with goods. In Tel Aviv we were threatened with a shortage of food. We had long dreamed of a port of our own. Now it became an urgent necessity. The government gave permission to build only a small jetty and provided no funds. The jetty was erected largely by volunteer labor on the part of the men of the city.

"The people of Tel Aviv then decided that we must have a real port of our own even though it was necessary to build it ourselves. It was estimated that the cost of a freight port would be $350,000. But where was the money to come from? The mayor issued a call. The response was astonishing. In five days the amount was subscribed by the people of Tel Aviv. Later, engineering experts found that a port adequate to our needs would cost nearly a million dollars, and another $500,000 was quickly subscribed. It is the only port in the world built by the people of a city rather than by the government of a country.

"One pound ($5.00) share certificates were issued, and two-thirds of the stock was sold in single shares. My boy of ten has a share certificate in his name. It is framed and hangs on the wall of his room. An old Yemenite Jewish woman came with her savings of six pounds ($30.00) wrapped up in a napkin. She purchased six shares, saying, 'I want these for my little grandchildren: one for Isaac, one for Rebekah, one for Jacob,' and so on through the family list of good Hebrew names."

Mr. Nedivi said he felt confident that the new port would mean great things for the future of the city and of the land of Palestine. The Town Clerk had become so eloquent in telling the story of the difficulties overcome and the results achieved in the upbuilding of Tel Aviv that at the close of the interview I exclaimed, "You should have been a preacher!"

"Well," he replied, "my father was an ardent

Zionist and went up and down America lecturing on the subject."

We thanked Mr. Nedivi heartily for the interesting narrative of the city's growth, and for giving us so much of his time. Then I pulled two New Testaments out of my pocket, one in Hebrew and one in English, and offered them to him. He readily accepted both of them, saying, "The New Testament is by no means a strange book to me. My father knew it almost by heart and advised me to read it."

Earlier in the day, before our interview with Mr. Nedivi, my wife and I had enjoyed inspecting the new freight port of which the city is so proud. An official of the port showed us around and told us that only a year previous to our visit the site of the port was simply a stretch of rocks and sand. Today, concrete walls have been built out into the sea, barges have been constructed, a big warehouse has been erected, and customs offices have been opened. While we were looking on, barges laden with cargo were plying to and from a steamer of the American Export Line anchored out in deeper water.

The building of Tel Aviv and of the new harbor is just another example of the fortitude and hope-filled labor of the Jews in a home of their own after their long centuries of wandering, and their determination to develop their home in Palestine to the utmost of their strength and power.

What has been accomplished at Tel Aviv in a few short years is just a picture in miniature of the future glory and greatness of the land of Palestine, as the Lord of Hosts overrules all obstacles and the Jews flock back in ever-increasing numbers to the heritage of their forefathers. In the years to come the prophecy of Ezekiel, uttered twenty-five centuries ago, will be fulfilled in ever larger and larger measure: "I will settle you after your old estates, and will do better unto you than at your beginnings: and ye shall know that I am the Lord."

CHAPTER V

MAKING PALESTINE AN AIRWAY CENTER

From a geographic point of view Palestine occupies a place of strategic importance. The country has been called the center of the earth's surface. It is the gateway between the Orient and the Occident. Hence it is not surprising that in the development of modern air routes Palestine should become an airway center.

The site selected for the Palestine airport is a large stretch of level ground near ancient Lydda. We read of Lydda in the New Testament. It was there that Peter healed Aeneas, and we are told that "all that dwelt at Lydda" seeing the man that was healed "turned to the Lord."

Today Lydda is a Mohammedan town, with probably few or no Christian inhabitants. It is unprogressive and unattractive. A curious feature of Lydda is the number of unfinished buildings on the main street. Some years ago, probably when the railway came to Lydda, these shops were partly built, but were left uncompleted. The attempt at progress did not succeed, and the town sank again into oriental languor.

FULFILLED IN PALESTINE

The airport near Lydda is in striking contrast to the town. It is up-to-date to the last degree. The situation of the airport is excellent from the traveler's standpoint. It is about a dozen miles from both Tel Aviv and Jaffa, and some thirty miles from Jerusalem.

A friend in Jerusalem spoke so enthusiastically about the new airport that I was eager to see it. He increased my interest by saying that a new and larger Royal Dutch Mail airplane would shortly be stopping there. We arranged to go to Lydda, and on the appointed day left Jerusalem by car. We reached the airport well before the hour set for the arrival of the Dutch plane. Just as we came to the flying field a plane of the Egyptian Airway Service hovered over the field, made a graceful landing, and rolled into the hangar to await the appointed time for another flight.

While waiting for the Dutch plane my friend introduced me to the engineer who constructed the runways for the landing of the planes, and who is erecting the airport building. The engineer was very kind in taking me over the runway and in giving information about the port.

The discovery was soon made that the runway at Lydda is one of the finest in the East. In fact it is probably not greatly excelled by many landing places in the world. Previous to that day I had supposed that the runway on which planes landed at an airport was simply a smooth piece of ground in a field. To my surprise I found it was far more complicated and costly than smooth soil.

There are four runways at the Lydda airport. Each is half a mile long and 330 feet wide. A force of 750 men worked for over a year constructing the runways and roads of the port. The runways are built of asphalt. An extensive drainage system had to be built to prevent rain water from getting under the asphalt and causing it to crack. The cost of the runways at the Lydda airport was nearly a million dollars!

The central airport building is now being constructed. It will cost another quarter of a million, and will contain a restaurant and sleeping accommodations; as well as immigration, customs, quarantine, and police offices.

Presently the big Dutch plane hove in sight. It circled round, dropped gently onto the runway, ran along it a considerable distance, and came to a stop not far from where I was standing. The plane was made of aluminum and glistened in the sunlight like a great silver-gray bird. The new Dutch machines are monoplanes, and are very fast. The regular schedule of the planes

DUTCH AIRPLANE LANDING AT LYDDA

One of the aluminum airplanes that make the long journey from Amsterdam, Holland, to Batavia, in Netherland East Indies, via Palestine.

between Amsterdam in Holland and Batavia in Java is five and a half days. Once, however, in a special contest the long journey of more than 9000 miles was completed in two days and four hours!

After the passengers had disembarked with their baggage I had the privilege of inspecting the machine. The Dutch wireless operator was very courteous and gladly gave me information. The big plane was a Douglas machine made in Santa Monica, California, and cost $150,000. The plane carries about fifteen passengers. I tried one of the seats and found it very comfortable. I then went into the engine room and found it a maze of buttons, and bulbs, and control apparatus.

The wireless operator said that each plane carries a crew of four: the captain, the first officer, the engineer, and the wireless operator. The plane—the wireless man called it a "ship"—is equipped with an automatic pilot. It is set for the course the plane is to take, and then simply adjusted a bit until the destination is reached. The ship is heated and the temperature is automatically regulated by a thermostat. The wireless man said that another valuable asset of the new machines is that they are almost sound proof. He declared passengers could carry on a conversation as easily while the plane was in motion as we were doing when the engine was shut off.

The operator evidently enjoyed flying and his own wireless work. He said he had been flying for five years, had never been in an accident, and felt just as safe in the air as on the land. The day previous, while flying over the Balkans, he had been in touch by wireless first with Amsterdam and, five minutes later, with Batavia, in Java, on the other side of the world.

As the time drew near for the plane to depart other officers appeared and stood chatting beside the ship. One of the officers told of the widely scattered places in which they take their meals. He said they had breakfast that morning in Athens and cool drinks at Alexandria. They had just had their lunch here at Lydda, and expected to have tea at Bagdad and supper in Bosrah! What could give one a better idea of the distances covered by these fast planes!

Presently the big plane was ready to take off for another flight. As it ran along the runway, and soared slowly and gracefully aloft, I felt for the first time in my life a longing to travel in the air. I was so intent on watching the machine that I had not noticed a young man standing beside me, until I heard him saying, "They shall mount up with wings as eagles."

Turning to him, I said, "You evidently know your Bible."

"Well," he replied, "I know it a bit."

Further conversation revealed the fact that he was a Jew, and the third generation of his family born in Palestine. We began to talk about conditions in the country, and he exclaimed, "What I can't understand is why we should be having so much trouble here in Palestine! We have come from other parts of the world expecting to find a haven of rest in this land. And now we have great trouble right here!"

I sympathized with his problem and sought to show him the explanation. Briefly I told him how long ago the sin of idolatry had been punished by exile and captivity in Babylon. Then the still greater sin that was committed when the nation rejected the Lord Jesus Christ—who had been foretold by all the Old Testament prophets—had been followed by a still longer exile that had already lasted nearly two thousand years. Today God in His great mercy is causing the Jews to return to their own land of Palestine, but, I told him, their troubles would never really be over until they as a nation acknowledge Jesus as their Messiah.

The young man seemed to assent in a measure to the statement that this sin was perhaps the

SLOWER THAN AN AIRPLANE
The camel has been aptly called the "ship of the desert."
It has been used for transportation in Palestine and the
orient for long centuries.

cause of their troubles, but he would not fully admit that Jesus was indeed the Messiah. At length I offered copies of the New Testament to the young man and his friend standing near, on condition that they would read them. Both assented, and willingly received the Life-giving Word. God grant that through reading His Word they may find forgiveness and peace and eternal life!

A little later we left the airport and made brief visits to Jaffa and Tel Aviv. We had been told that a Polish plane was due to reach Lydda that afternoon. We arrived back at the airport just in time to see the Polish plane descend gracefully onto the runway. It also was made of aluminum, and glistened brightly in the sunlight. Two of the passengers had flown from Helsingfors in Finland via Warsaw to Lydda in two days. They said they were quite comfortable in the reclining arm chairs, and that they felt perfectly safe throughout the journey. They declared the airport at Lydda was the best they had seen during their trip.

The airport at Lydda is a stopping place for the airlines of four nations. One is British—the Imperial Royal Airways that ply between different parts of the British Empire. Gaza had been their landing place, but they expected to join the

FULFILLED IN PALESTINE 65

other lines at Lydda very shortly. Another airline is Dutch—the K. L. M. or Royal Dutch Mail line whose planes go from Amsterdam to Batavia. A third airline is Polish—the planes flying from Warsaw to Lydda and return, Lydda being the terminus of the route. The fourth air highway is Egyptian—the planes plying between Cairo and Bagdad.

The air service between Egypt and Iraq, or ancient Assyria, with a landing field at Lydda, is just another link in the chain that is binding together more closely day by day three lands of the Near East: Palestine, Egypt and Iraq. A railway runs from Cairo to Haifa in Palestine, and large buses quickly cover the distance from Damascus to Bagdad.

These developments are all leading up to the complete fulfillment in the days to come of a very remarkable prediction made by the prophet Isaiah in chapter 19, verses 23 to 25: "In that day there shall be a highway out of Egypt to Assyria, and the Assyrian shall come into Egypt, and the Egyptian into Assyria, and the Egyptians shall serve with the Assyrians. In that day shall Israel be the third with Egypt and with Assyria, even a blessing in the midst of the land: whom the Lord of hosts shall bless, saying,

Blessed be Egypt my people, and Assyria the work of my hands, and Israel mine inheritance."

The air and rail and road highways that are linking up Egypt and Assyria are daily fulfilling the first part of the prophecy. But what of the second part? It is still future. It forecasts what will take place after the return of the Lord Jesus Christ to rule and reign over all the earth. "In that day" (verse 24), the Jews of Palestine will with one accord acknowledge that the Lord Jesus is indeed the long-promised Messiah; and the Mohammedans of Egypt and Iraq will know that Christ is not only "a prophet," but "the prophet," promised by Moses in Deuteronomy 18:18, and is the very Son of God! Then—*and not till then*—will the feud between the Jews and Mohammedans be healed. Then will they dwell together in peace and harmony and brotherly love, trusting in the Lord Jesus Christ as their Messiah, and Prophet, and Saviour, and King. And then will the prophecy of Isaiah be fulfilled in all its fullness: "Blessed be Egypt my people, and Assyria the work of my hands, and Israel mine inheritance."

CHAPTER VI

JERUSALEM THE TRANSFORMED

For centuries Jerusalem sat drowsing on the Judean hills. During the present generation she has been aroused from her long lethargy, and has taken on new life and vigor.

A remarkable transformation has taken place in the historic city. The Jerusalem of today is alert, modern, vibrant with life, and humming with business, educational, and political activity.

The old city within the walls, with its narrow streets and towering bulwarks, and sacred associations, still remains. For millions in many lands it is the most hallowed spot on earth. But the return of the Jews in recent years has made the old walled city only a small part of greater Jerusalem.

The new city outside the walls now occupies an area ten times as large as that of the old city! New Jerusalem has grown during the past few years with amazing rapidity. The population is now well over 100,000 people. It has busy wide thoroughfares, buses, electric lights and telephones, modern shops and public buildings, parks and playgrounds, and new suburbs with beautiful homes. It is becoming as advanced and up-to-date as a city in Europe or America.

The vice-mayor of Jerusalem recently gave a pen picture of the growing city. He said that the new influx of population "has given rise to the construction of new town quarters and garden suburbs, the creation of factories, workshops and business centers, the formation of a network of new schools and synagogues, the founding of hospitals and health centers, and the establishment of a university and several colleges of technical, musical, and art instruction."

Two streets in Jerusalem show the striking contrast between the old city and the new. One is David Street in the old city—a narrow, dark lane lined with oriental bazaars. The other is St. Julian's Way, a near-by street in the new city. It is wide, well paved, and lined with attractive shops and modern buildings. On this street is the million dollar Y. M. C. A. building, one of the architectural ornaments of the city, and directly opposite the "Y" stands the sumptuous King David Hotel.

The hostels of a city are often an index of its character. Two hotels especially interested us. They were built about half a century apart. One is called the "first" hotel of the city. Alas for

OLD WAYS IN JERUSALEM
A narrow street within the walls of the old city where customs have remained unchanged for centuries.

NEW WAYS IN JERUSALEM
Saint Julian's Way, one of the broad thoroughfares pulsing with modern traffic, in the newer section of the city.

those who had to lodge in that unattractive structure. The other hotel is the "King David," built by the owners of Shepheard's Hotel, Cairo. It is about the last word in luxury and elegance in hotel construction. What a contrast between the "first" and the "last"! It is typical of the transformation that has taken place in the city since the Jews have been streaming back into the city of their forefathers.

Various public buildings in Jerusalem would do credit to any modern city. One is the new Rockefeller Museum of Antiquities, which has been several years in building and has just been opened. It is a great stone structure north of the Temple area, and overlooking the Mount of Olives and Mount Scopus, the site of the new Hebrew University.

Another building that is just being completed, and of which the city may well be proud, is the new post office. It is located in the heart of the business district and commands a splendid view of Jerusalem looking southward. The post office is built of "Jerusalem hard-stone" quarried between Jerusalem and Bethlehem, and is decorated with black basalt from Magdala on the Sea of Galilee. A great hall in the building is being equipped with automatic telephones as the post office will be the telephone exchange not only for Jerusalem but for all the land of Palestine.

Plans are under way to make the Jerusalem of the future even more attractive and beautiful than it is today. In the providence of God, while Mrs. Davis and I were in Singapore en route to Palestine, a friend gave us a letter of introduction to a man in Jerusalem who proved to be the town planning advisor to the Palestine government. I also talked with the Jerusalem town planner. Both were most kind and cordial. It was a pleasure to learn that both the municipality of Jerusalem and the government of Palestine are eager to conserve three priceless landmarks that are of world-wide interest:

First, the old city within the walls, which is a hallowed spot for Christians, Jews, and Mohammedans.

Second, the centuries-old wall of the ancient city of Jerusalem, and the moat around it.

Third, the Mount of Olives that is mentioned so frequently in the Bible, and that was so loved by our Lord.

The Town Planning Advisor told us of the far-sightedness of Lord Allenby—the British general who captured Jerusalem without firing a single shot. He said that soon after he took possession of the city General Allenby issued orders that the walls of Jerusalem should be preserved; that no buildings should be erected on the moat space along the north wall; and he prohibited the putting up of buildings on the Mount of Olives. Later the enforcement of the restrictions became somewhat lax, and some Arab houses were built on the Mount, but now litigation is in progress to have them taken away.

Today a considerable part of the western wall of the old city is hidden from view by the shops along one side of Jaffa road. As a matter of fact we had spent several weeks in Jerusalem before we caught a glimpse of this part of the wall behind the shops. No repairs are allowed to be made on these buildings. Ere long they are to be torn down so that this portion of the ancient wall may be seen in all its sturdy grandeur.

We were greatly interested in learning from the Town Planning Advisor that the walls of Jerusalem are really higher than they seem to be from the portion that is now visible. He told us that in 1867 the Warren Expedition from the United States made excavations at the southeastern corner of the city, and discovered that only about one third of the height of the wall was exposed to view. He said they are planning to dig away the debris of centuries that has ac-

A Jerusalem Hotel of Fifty Years Ago
The "first hotel" in Jerusalem, built before the Jews returned in large numbers from their long exile.

A Jerusalem Hotel of Today
The "King David," a luxurious modern hotel in the new section of the city.

cumulated around the walls of Jerusalem. The ancient moat will then be seen, and the walls will stand out with still greater boldness and beauty.

The Advisor told us of several projects they are planning to carry out for the further adornment of Jerusalem: One of the plans includes the construction of a beautiful wide boulevard around Jerusalem. It is to encircle the city on the west and north, and to run along the top of the Mount of Olives on the east. It is to be one hundred or more feet in width, and to have a double roadway, with trees planted on both sides of the boulevard. Another plan is to make a large park at the southern end of the city. Land has already been reserved for this project.

General Allenby's order against erecting buildings on the Mount of Olives is to be supplemented by making the Mount a national reservation. It will, however, take time and money to carry out this project. First of all a fund of millions of dollars will be required to compensate those who have purchased land on the Mount. It is planned to make terraces on the side that faces Jerusalem, and to plant many more olive trees, and so make the Mount true to its name.

It is a merciful providence that building operations on the Mount of Olives have been prohibited. The loss of hundreds or thousands of

FULFILLED IN PALESTINE

lives will thus be averted in view of the coming earthquake that is to cleave the mountain asunder. In Zechariah 14: 4 we read: "And his feet shall stand in that day upon the mount of Olives, which is before Jerusalem on the east, and the mount of Olives shall cleave in the midst thereof toward the east and toward the west, and there shall be a very great valley; and half of the mountain shall remove toward the north, and half of it toward the south."

During recent years earthquakes have severely damaged buildings on the famous Mount. At the northern end of the Mount stands the palace built by Ex-Emperor William of Germany. An earthquake in 1927 rocked this building and greatly damaged it. We were told of a curious thing that happened to one part of the building. In a great room of the palace there was a picture in mosaic of Emperor William and his wife seated on thrones and holding between them a miniature replica of the palace. Strangely enough the earthquake shattered the miniature palace out of their hands! The great palace has been partially repaired, and is at present used as a barracks for British troops.

But the greatest earthquake of all is yet future, and will take place exactly as predicted by the prophet Zechariah. The geological formation of the soil of the Mount of Olives is all set for the coming event. It only awaits God's appointed moment to act. Professor Bailey Willis, the seismological expert of Leland Stanford University, made this striking statement before the British Association for the Advancement of Science: "The region around Jerusalem is a region of potential earthquake danger. A 'fault line,' along which an earth slippage may occur at any time, passes directly through the Mount of Olives."

Twenty-five centuries after the prophecy was uttered, science confirms the probability of the foretold event!

The cleavage of the Mount of Olives is to be followed by another remarkable change. It is foretold in Zechariah 14:8: "And it shall be in that day, that living waters shall go out from Jerusalem; half of them toward the former sea, and half of them toward the hinder sea: in summer and in winter shall it be."

One day, during our stay in Jerusalem, a friend was showing Mrs. Davis and myself the Temple Area on which the Dome of the Rock now stands. He told us that the late Lord Kitchener, when a lieutenant, spent some time in Palestine making surveys in connection with the Palestine Exploration Society. He said Lord

OLD AND NEW JERUSALEM

The foreground shows the ancient walls and the Dome of the Rock. In the distance are seen modern buildings of the new section of Jerusalem.

Kitchener was convinced, from his researches, that there was a considerable body of water under the city. It is possible that this underground lake or river may become the source of the predicted flow of "living waters" from Jerusalem.

And simultaneously with these physical convulsions of nature, a far greater event will take place, toward which the prophets have been pointing for thousands of years. It is the return of the Lord Jesus Christ, the long-promised Messiah, to rule and reign over all the peoples and nations of the earth. In the same chapter of Zechariah, in the verse following the one just quoted, the prophet forecasts the rule of the King: "And the Lord shall be king over all the earth: in that day shall there be one Lord, and his name one."

Long ago the Lord Jesus came in lowliness and meekness to offer Himself as a sacrificial Lamb for the sins of the world. But soon He is coming to this earth again—not this time in humility, but in majesty. He is coming as a King in the clouds of heaven, and will rule and reign over all the earth as King of kings, and Lord of lords. The seat of His Kingdom will be Jerusalem, the city that is now being adorned and beautified and made ready for the coming of the Messiah, the King.

CHAPTER VII

WHO OWNS PALESTINE?

Who owns Palestine?

It is impossible to have a clear conception of conditions in Palestine until this vital question has been faced and answered.

The British justly claim authority over the country because they wrested it from the Turks during the World War. The Arabs declare the land is theirs by virtue of actual occupation for they and their ancestors have lived in it for long centuries past.

But who really holds the title deed to the land of Palestine?

The answer to the question dates back not to the British or Turkish or Moslem conquests of the country; nor to the several centuries of occupation by the Arabs. The question of ownership was settled thousands of years previous to any of these events. Nearly 4000 years ago the Lord God of Hosts, the Creator and Possessor of heaven and earth, expressly deeded the land to Abraham and to his seed forever!

The account of the transaction is given in Genesis 13, verses 14, 15, and 17: "And the Lord said unto Abram, after that Lot was separated from him, Lift up now thine eyes, and look from the place where thou art northward, and southward, and eastward, and westward: for all the land which thou seest, to thee will I give it, and to thy seed for ever. . . . Arise, walk through the land in the length of it and in the breadth of it; for I will give it unto thee."

Some years later God spoke again to Abram, and made a solemn covenant with him, and enlarged the boundaries of the land that should ultimately belong to his descendants. The limits of the greater possession are given in Genesis 15:18: "In the same day the Lord made a covenant with Abram, saying, Unto thy seed have I given this land, from the river of Egypt unto the great river, the river Euphrates."

The "river of Egypt" is a small stream at the southern boundary of Canaan, bordering on the wilderness of Paran. The territory from this southern extremity of Palestine to the river Euphrates includes a great expanse of land many times the size of ancient Canaan. It is now largely a bleak, barren desert. But if irrigated and cultivated it might well become a modern garden of Eden, and could accommodate several times the 15,000,000 Jews in the world today.

When Abraham was ninety and nine years old God appeared to him and talked with him once more of the covenant, telling him that it was an everlasting covenant and that the land would be an everlasting possession. In Genesis 17, verses 7 and 8, God spoke to Abraham saying: "And I will establish my covenant between me and thee and thy seed after thee in their generations for an everlasting covenant, to be a God unto thee, and to thy seed after thee. And I will give unto thee, and to thy seed after thee, the land wherein thou art a stranger, all the land of Canaan, for an everlasting possession; and I will be their God."

The thrice repeated covenant which God had made with Abraham was confirmed to Isaac. The promise to Isaac is recorded in Genesis 26, verses 3 and 4: "Sojourn in this land, and I will be with thee, and will bless thee; for unto thee, and unto thy seed, I will give all these countries, and I will perform the oath which I sware unto Abraham thy father; and I will make thy seed to multiply as the stars of heaven, and will give unto thy seed all these countries; and in thy seed shall all the nations of the earth be blessed."

Isaac never forgot God's promise. When he was an old man he reminded his son Jacob of it as he blessed him and sent him away. As Jacob journeyed and came to Bethel, God appeared to him in a dream and renewed the covenant. The story is given in Genesis 28: 12 to 14: "And he dreamed, and behold a ladder set up on the earth, and the top of it reached to heaven: and behold the angels of God ascending and descending on it. And, behold, the Lord stood above it, and said, I am the Lord God of Abraham thy father, and the God of Isaac: the land whereon thou liest, to thee will I give it, and to thy seed; and thy seed shall be as the dust of the earth, and thou shalt spread abroad to the west, and to the east, and to the north, and to the south: and in thee and in thy seed shall all the families of the earth be blessed."

It is necessary to keep clearly in mind that while the gift of the land to Abraham, Isaac, and Jacob, and to their seed, was complete and unconditional, yet Israel's actual occupation of the territory deeded to them was an entirely different matter. Centuries after the covenant was made, Moses told the children of Israel that if they obeyed the commandments of the Lord they would be prosperous and happy and would dwell safely in the land God had given them. However, if they disobeyed Him they would be scattered to the ends of the earth and become a reproach among all nations.

FROM SWAMP TO FLOURISHING COLONY

The colony of Nahalal is situated on land which was once swampy and infested with mosquitoes. Today it is one of the garden spots of Palestine.

This prediction of Moses is one of the most daring forecasts ever made in the history of the human race. Think of it! A great leader telling his fellow countrymen, when they had not yet entered the promised land, what would happen to the nation thousands of years later! Through the inspiration of the Almighty, Moses looked down through the long corridor of time, and predicted with unerring precision both the blessings of obedience and the disasters of disobedience. The manner in which the prophecies of the 28th chapter of Deuteronomy have been fulfilled during the nearly 3,500 years since they were uttered, proves beyond any peradventure of doubt, the supernatural inspiration of the Bible!

In Deuteronomy 28: 1-13, Moses gives a glowing picture of the future greatness and prosperity of the children of Israel, that would follow their keeping the commandments of their God. History records the remarkable manner in which these predictions were fulfilled. Under David and Solomon the people kept God's commandments. The nation prospered and the people dwelt safely in their own land. Further, the boundaries of their dominion were extended far beyond the land of Canaan and embraced the enlarged territory promised to Abraham in Genesis 15, "from the river of Egypt unto the great river, the river Euphrates."

And we know from God's Word that in the days to come, under the rule of King David's greater Son, the Lord Jesus Christ, the boundaries of Israel's territory will extend from the river of Egypt to the Euphrates; while the dominion and sway of the King of kings will be that foretold in Psalm 72, "from sea to sea, and from the river unto the ends of the earth . . . Yea, all kings shall fall down before him: all nations shall serve him."

Now let us see what Moses predicted would befall the Israelites if they failed to obey the Lord their God. Moses' prediction of punishment is one of the most terrible pictures of human misery and suffering recorded in the world's literature. It occupies the last 54 verses of the 28th chapter of Deuteronomy. It is summarized in verses 63 to 67: "And it shall come to pass, that as the Lord rejoiced over you to do you good, and to multiply you; so the Lord will rejoice over you to destroy you, and to bring you to nought; and ye shall be plucked from off the land whither thou goest to possess it. And the Lord shall scatter thee among all people, from the one end of the earth even unto the other; and there thou shalt serve other gods, which neither thou nor thy fathers have known, even wood and stone. And among these nations shalt thou find no ease, neither shall the sole of thy foot have rest: but the Lord shall give thee there a trembling heart, and failing of eyes, and sorrow of mind: and thy life shall hang in doubt before thee; and thou shalt fear day and night, and shalt have none assurance of thy life: in the morning thou shalt say, Would God it were even! and at even thou shalt say, Would God it were morning! for the fear of thine heart wherewith thou shalt fear, and for the sight of thine eyes which thou shalt see."

Just as the predictions of blessing were fulfilled to the letter, so this prophecy of punishment for disobedience has been fulfilled with the same precision. In the latter part of King Solomon's reign idolatry increased rapidly among the children of Israel. Multiplied warnings and threats of impending disaster were uttered by the prophets but to no avail. Finally judgment fell. Jerusalem was captured; Solomon's temple was destroyed; and the people were carried captive into the land of their enemies.

The captivity lasted 70 years just as foretold by the prophet Jeremiah (Jeremiah 25:11 and 12). The fervent prayers of Daniel and Nehemiah in the country of their captivity prevailed.

FROM BARRENNESS TO BEAUTY
More than a million trees have been planted by the Jews. The hills are being transformed from barrenness to beauty.

CATTLE AT THE RIVER KISHON
Long ago the prophetess Deborah sang of "that ancient river, the river Kishon."

Tens of thousands of Israelites returned to the land of their fathers. Those years of chastening in idolatrous Babylon were not in vain for the Jews forever after abhorred idols with all their heart and soul.

For several centuries the Jews dwelt in their own land, and grew and multiplied until the time of our Lord's earthly ministry. But once again they had wandered far from their God. Hypocrisy and greed and immorality were rampant. Our Lord termed the people of His day, "an evil and adulterous generation." Little wonder, with their eyes blinded by sin, they failed to realize that the One who healed the sick, and raised the dead, and "spake as never man spake," was their long promised Messiah!

Their rulers rejected and caused to be crucified the Son of David, the Servant of Jehovah, whose advent and life and death and resurrection had been foretold in detail by the Old Testament prophets. How swiftly judgment fell! In less than fifty years after the rejection, Jerusalem was destroyed, the magnificent temple built by Herod was burned to the ground, and the Jews were scattered, this time not to Babylon, but "among all people, from the one end of the earth unto the other"—precisely as predicted by Moses 1500 years before!

FULFILLED IN PALESTINE

The second captivity has continued for more than eighteen centuries. But long ago the Old Testament prophets, Isaiah, Jeremiah, Ezekiel and others, predicted that in the latter days the Jews would return to their own land. Many of these prophecies have both a near and far fulfillment, referring first to the return from Babylon and then to that greater return out of all countries whither the children of Israel have been scattered. It is this greater return that we are witnessing in this generation before our very eyes.

It is estimated that there are in Palestine today some 430,000 Jews. This is about ten times as many as returned from the Babylonian captivity under Ezra and Nehemiah. When the children of Israel returned to Palestine after 70 years absence, they found Jerusalem in ruins and others in possession of the country. So in recent years as they have been streaming back to their ancient heritage from all parts of the world, they again have found the land largely waste and desolate, and others dwelling in it.

The question naturally arises, "What about the Arabs now living in Palestine? Are they to be dispossessed and driven out?" The answer is very clear. In all the negotiations for making a national home for the Jews in Palestine, the rights of the non-Jewish people of the country have never been questioned. Both the Balfour Declaration and the Mandate, given Great Britain by the League of Nations, fully guarantee the civil and religious rights of the people now dwelling in the land. The exact words of the Balfour Declaration are these: "Nothing shall be done to prejudice the civil and religious rights of existing non-Jewish communities in Palestine."

This principle of equal rights has been accepted by the Jews in their plans for the establishment of a national home in Palestine. During our stay in Jerusalem, Mrs. Davis and I called on one of the leaders of the Jewish Agency, the organization that is assisting Jews throughout the world to return to Palestine. He stated the principle in no uncertain terms: "We wish to live here on the basis of equality, with no domination of Jews over Arabs or Arabs over Jews. We want equal rights for all, entirely irrespective of the numbers of either race."

But on the matter of "Who owns Palestine" the Jewish leader was equally clear and unequivocal. With fervor he exclaimed: "Palestine is to us the soul of our life! We have been attached to the land by Divine Providence, and what God hath joined together no man can put asunder! The Jews alone can bring the land back to life for it belongs to them!"

God has never revoked the solemn covenant that He made with Abraham nearly 4000 years ago in which He expressly deeded the land to the patriarch and to his seed forever. From that day to this he has never cancelled the title-deed. A thousand years after the time of Abraham, the Psalmist reiterated the covenant: "He hath remembered his covenant for ever, the word which he commanded to a thousand generations. Which covenant he made with Abraham, and his oath unto Isaac; and confirmed the same unto Jacob for a law, and to Israel for an everlasting covenant: saying, Unto thee will I give the land of Canaan, the lot of your inheritance: when they were but a few men in number; yea, very few, and strangers in it". (Psalm 105: 8-12).

Palestine is the "lot" of Israel's inheritance today just as truly as it was long ago when Moses and the Psalmist recorded the divine transaction. When God makes a promise it is final and irrevocable. His Word is "for ever settled in heaven."

For long centuries disobedience has deprived the Jews of the privilege of occupying Palestine. Today by divine grace they are returning and dwelling in a portion of the land, but the title-deed to the entire country still rests safely in their name in the vaults of heaven!

Chapter VIII

THE NEHEMIAH OF MODERN PALESTINE

Long ago God called a cupbearer at the court of King Artaxerxes of Persia, and used him as His instrument to rebuild Jerusalem that had lain waste and desolate 70 years.

In our own generation God called a chemist in an English University, and commissioned him to play a leading part in rebuilding, not merely Jerusalem, but the land of Palestine that had lain waste and desolate for long centuries.

Both stories of reconstruction show in an unmistakable manner the hand of God working on behalf of His chosen people the Jews. The careers of Nehemiah of old, and his modern counterpart, reveal anew the principle that when God calls a man to accomplish a task, He equips him with the necessary qualities to carry the matter through to a successful completion.

The Nehemiah of today is Dr. Chaim Weizmann, president of the world Zionist movement. He is also president of the Jewish Agency, the organization that is chiefly responsible for the rehabilitation of Palestine. Dr. Weizmann was

FULFILLED IN PALESTINE

born in Russia; received his inspiration for Zionism from Theodore Herzl; eloquently championed its cause in Europe; awakened deep interest in Zionism in Lord Balfour and Lloyd George; and stirred the souls of both men to help in securing a homeland for the Jews in Palestine. Since the attainment of that object he has traveled throughout the world organizing the Jews of many lands to co-operate financially in the reconstruction of their ancient heritage.

Dr. Weizmann has a home in Palestine, and loves to be there when not urgently needed elsewhere. When Mrs. Davis and I visited the Agricultural Experiment Station at Rehovoth, they showed us the home of Dr. Weizmann. It is beautifully situated on a knoll not far distant from the agricultural station. As a chemist the Jewish leader is greatly interested in the experiments that are being carried on to secure the largest possible production from each acre of soil in Palestine. He realizes that the more each acre produces, the larger the number of colonists that can be settled on the land.

Dr. Weizmann's life has been almost as full of providential guidance as that of his famous predecessor of long ago. In 1906 Dr. Weizmann was a lecturer in organic chemistry at Manchester University in England. His soul was aflame with a passionate longing that the land of Palestine might somehow be thrown open for settlement to the Jews of the world. But there was small prospect of such an event at that time, for the country was still under the iron rule of the Turks.

At that time the Hon. Arthur J. Balfour, one of the outstanding British statesmen of the last generation, was in Manchester in the white heat of a political campaign. Mr. Balfour was exceedingly busy with his speaking engagements. He was, however, greatly interested to know why it was that the Jews had rejected an offer of the British Government to give them a homeland in British East Africa. Mr. Balfour mentioned his interest to a friend, and was told that one of the younger leaders of Zionism was a lecturer on chemistry at Manchester University. Mr. Balfour asked to see him. An interview was arranged to last fifteen minutes. The conversation, however, went on for an hour and a quarter, during which the young chemist explained to the British statesman the aims and aspirations of the Zionist movement. He showed him that the land of Palestine was the only national home that would appeal to the Jews throughout the world. It was one of those meetings of two strong personalities that sometimes have epoch making results. In speaking of that memorable interview, Mrs. Blanche E. Dugdale, the biographer of Lord Balfour, and who was also his niece, says that in years to come it was "to bear fruit undreamed of by them both, and to set its impress upon history, in the Balfour Declaration of 1917, pledging the British Government to promote the establishment of a national home for the Jews in Palestine."

That meeting in Manchester marked the beginning of a life-long friendship between the two men. When the Balfour pronouncement about Palestine was in the making the two men were in close communication. Lord Balfour had been completely won over to the cause of Zionism. In 1925, eight years after the appearance of the historic Balfour Declaration, the British statesman accompanied Dr. and Mrs. Weizmann on a visit to Palestine to attend the opening of the Hebrew University. The day the party arrived in Jerusalem, the Arab newspapers appeared in black borders to express their feelings of dislike toward the statesman-friend of the Jews. However, the lack of welcome on the part of the Arabs was abundantly atoned for by the joyous demonstrations of the Jews. At Tel Aviv cheering crowds thronged the streets. Everywhere Lord

Balfour went in Palestine he was received with unbounded enthusiasm.

The friendship between the Jewish leader and the British statesman lasted until the death of the latter. A few days before Lord Balfour's death, Dr. Weizmann was admitted to his bedside. No words passed between them, for Lord Balfour was very weak, but there was the same sympathetic bond of union between them that had begun in that memorable meeting in Manchester in 1906.

Let me say in passing that Lord Balfour was not only a great statesman, but a great Christian thinker and philosopher. Mrs. Dugdale, his biographer, states that nothing was more woven into the texture of his being than his belief in the existence of a personal God—"a God who answers prayer." Mrs. Dugdale also records the fact that near the end of his life Lord Balfour told her that "what he had been able to do for the Jews had been the thing he looked back upon as the most worth his doing."

Dr. Weizmann's friendship with the British statesman had no small influence in the securing of a national homeland for the Jews. But another providential event had occurred in the life of the Jewish chemist that was destined to have a very vital connection with the return of the Jewish people to Palestine.

JEWISH IMMIGRANTS LANDING AT JAFFA

The newcomers are chiefly from Germany. They are eager to disembark and have a share in rebuilding Palestine.

It was a time of crisis during the World War. Lloyd George was Minister of Munitions before he became the Premier of Great Britain. A certain chemical, called acetone, was an essential element in the making of cordite for manufacturing small and great cartridges. The supply of acetone was running dangerously low. Great Britain could not produce it in sufficient quantities, and it was extremely difficult to get it from America. It was a critical situation for Britain and the Allies, but in the providence of God there was one man who was destined to overcome the crisis, and he was a Jew.

In one of the six volumes of his war memoirs Lloyd George tells the story of what happened. In his characteristically clear and lucid style he says:

"I was confronted by a serious crisis. It became clear that the supplies of wood alcohol for the manufacture of acetone would prove quite insufficient to meet the increasing demands, particularly in 1916. The matter was urgent, for without the acetone there would be no cordite for our cartridges, for either rifles or big guns."

At that time Lloyd George told the late editor of the Manchester Guardian of his difficulty, and said he was looking for a resourceful chemist who would help to solve the problem. The editor said to Lloyd George: "There is a very remarkable professor of chemistry in the University of Manchester who is willing to place his services at the disposal of the State."

The Minister of Munitions lost no time in getting in touch with this chemist. Lloyd George tells the story of their meeting and of how much he was impressed with the Zionist leader and chemist.

"I took his word about Professor Weizmann and invited him to London to see me. I took to him at once. He is now a man of international fame. He was then quite unknown to the general public, but as soon as I met him I realized that he was a very remarkable personality. His brow gave assurance of a fine intellect, and his open countenance gave confidence in his complete sincerity.

"I told him we were in a chemical dilemma and asked him to assist us. I explained the shortage in wood alcohol and what it meant in munitionment. Could he help? Dr. Weizmann said he did not know, but he would try. He could produce acetone on a laboratory scale, but it would require some time before he could guarantee successful production on a manufacturing scale.

" 'How long can you give me?' he asked.

"I said, 'I cannot give you very long. It is pressing.'

"Weizmann replied, 'I will go at it night and day.'

"In a few weeks' time he came to me and said 'The problem is solved.'

"When our difficulties were solved through Dr. Weizmann's genius, I said to him: 'You have rendered great service to the State, and I should like to ask the Prime Minister to recommend you to His Majesty for some honor.'

"He said: 'There is nothing I want for myself.'

" 'But is there nothing we can do as a recognition of your valuable services to the country?' I asked.

"He replied, 'Yes, I would like you to do something for my people.' He then explained his aspirations as to the repatriation of the Jews to the sacred land they had made famous."

How this conversation carries one back through the centuries to the time when Nehemiah stood before King Artaxerxes ready to give him the cup of wine. Seeing the sad countenance of the cupbearer the king inquired the cause, and Nehemiah replied: "Why should not my countenance be sad, when the city, the place of my fathers' sepulchres, lieth waste, and the gates thereof are consumed with fire?

FULFILLED IN PALESTINE 101

"Then the king said unto me, For what dost thou make request? So I prayed to the God of heaven.

"And I said unto the king, If it please the king, and if thy servant have found favor in thy sight, that thou wouldest send me unto Judah, unto the city of my fathers' sepulchres, that I may build it."

The king granted the request of Nehemiah, and the story of his rebuilding the wall of Jerusalem in the face of great opposition is one of the heroic chapters in the long and varied history of the Jews.

Now let us continue the story of the modern Nehemiah. Lloyd George goes on to say: "As soon as I became Prime Minister I talked the whole matter over with Mr. Balfour, who was then Foreign Secretary. As a scientist he was immensely interested when I told him of Dr. Weizmann's achievement. Dr. Weizmann was brought into direct contact with the Foreign Secretary.

"The outcome, after long examination, was the famous Balfour Declaration, which became the charter of the Zionist movement. So Dr. Weizmann with his discovery not only helped us to win the war, but made a permanent mark upon the map of the world."

In speaking of the activities of the Zionist leader after the Mandate over Palestine had become a reality, Lloyd George said: "Dr. Weizmann is still the same busy, devoted, self-forgetful enthusiast. When I saw him recently he had just returned from a collecting tour abroad for the Zionist cause, in which he raised 70,000 pounds ($350,000). He has collected something like fifteen or sixteen million pounds sterling ($75,000,000 to $80,000,000) for the rebuilding of Zion. It is the only reward he seeks, and his name will rank with that of Nehemiah in the fascinating and inspiring story of the Children of Israel."

Dr. Weizmann is God's chosen instrument in helping to bring into being a homeland for the Jews, and in assisting in building it up. In view of his invaluable services it is very fitting that Dr. Weizmann's fellow countrymen should have made him the head both of the Zionist movement and of the Jewish Agency.

Just as long ago the Lord called His servant Nehemiah, and led him on step by step in the difficult task of rebuilding the walls of Jerusalem; so in our day God has chosen a modern Nehemiah, and has led him forward from one event to another, to help in accomplishing the divine purpose in the reconstruction of the land of Palestine.

Chapter IX

THE PARTITION OF PALESTINE

Will the partition of Palestine be a bane or a blessing? Will it bring peace or further discord to that strife-torn country?

These are the questions that are being discussed by Christians and Jews and Arabs throughout the world.

The Royal Commission, sent by the British Government to inquire into the causes of the disorders in Palestine, have reported that the British Mandate over the country cannot be successfully carried out and should be abrogated. They have advocated a new order of things in that ancient land. They have declared that the partition of Palestine is the one thing that will insure permanent peace between the Jews and Arabs.

The Royal Commission spent weeks in Palestine interviewing Jews and Arabs, and securing facts regarding the underlying causes of the troubles between the two races. Then they returned to Great Britain and spent months sifting the information, and formulating a solution that would inaugurate a new era of peace and harmony.

With intense eagerness the world awaited the report of the Commission, for it might mean a new and eventful chapter in the long and varied history of Palestine. At length the report was made public. It was a volume of 400 pages. Newspapers throughout the world published lengthy extracts from it. The New York Times gave four news pages to the report, and carried an editorial two columns long discussing its merits and demerits.

It is small wonder that the report aroused world-wide discussion, for it suggested drastic changes in the methods of governing Palestine. The following are some of the proposals put forward in the report:

First: That the British Mandate over Palestine was unworkable, and should be abrogated.

Second: That Palestine should be divided into two independent states, one Jewish and the other Arab.

Third: That certain sacred cities and places, such as Jerusalem, Bethlehem, Nazareth, and the district around the Sea of Galilee, should not be included in either the Jewish or the Arab states, but should be neutral, remaining under a permanent mandate, preferably British.

FULFILLED IN PALESTINE

Fourth: That there should be a neutral corridor of land extending from Jerusalem to Jaffa on the Mediterranean seacoast.

These were some of the many suggestions put forth by the Commission as the only possible solution of the Palestine problem. Some hailed the report as a wise proposal that would usher in a new era of peace and good will between the two races. Others were equally emphatic in expressing their condemnation of the report.

Multitudes of Jews throughout the world were well-nigh heartbroken by the report. It seemed to shatter their hopes and dreams of a national home in the land of their forefathers. One of the strongest criticisms was that the amount of land offered to the Jews in the Royal Commission report was almost a miniature of the original territory promised them by the Balfour Declaration. Under the original Mandate the territory designated for the Jewish homeland included Transjordania as well as Palestine. Later, Transjordania was made an Arab territory with Emir Abdullah as its ruler. This action automatically shut out Jewish immigration to that area which is far greater than that of Palestine. And now, less than 20 years later, the Commission was suggesting that little Palestine be divided into two or three parts, and the smaller portion of it given to the Jews! Thus the land offered to the Jews in the report of the Commission is about five per cent of the area originally covered by the Mandate!

Another criticism of the report was that the land offered to the Jews for a state of their own was already largely settled. Most of this land had been purchased from the Arabs and had been colonized and cultivated during the past few years. What the Jews now needed was a large barren waste, like the big Beersheba district, so that new immigrants could settle there and transform it from a wilderness to a garden of Eden as had been done in other parts of Palestine.

The need of the Jews for a larger area than that suggested by the Commission is imperative. Millions of Jews in Europe are being persecuted, and are in dire distress, and an outlet for them must be secured. Palestine is the logical and natural place of refuge from the increasing waves of anti-Semitism. In the face of this serious situation why were the Jews offered such a small territory?

One of the recommendations of the report that brought consternation to Jews in all parts of the world was the proposal to limit immigration into Palestine during the next five years to a maximum number of 12,000 annually! In other words, it would almost stop the stream of Jewish immigration that had been flowing so freely into Palestine during the past few years.

But the proposal that brought most poignant sorrow to the Jews everywhere was the suggestion that Jerusalem should be outside the pale of the proposed Jewish state. The Chief Rabbi of Palestine, Dr. Isaac Herzog, published a stirring rejoinder to this proposal:

"For millions of Jews the only glimmer of hope in their lives, embittered by appalling economic distress and utterly darkened by relentless persecution, has been the future national home. The climax of the shock is reached when we see Jerusalem—inexpressibly dear to every Jewish heart—cut out of the proposed Jewish dwarf state. On the banks of the rivers of Babylon our forefathers, exiled from Zion—virtually another name for Jerusalem and also a synonym for Palestine—solemnly swore: 'If I forget thee, oh, Jerusalem, let my right hand forget its cunning.' ... In our prayers, private, public, thrice daily, and in the grace after meals, we pray for Jerusalem. The inspiring service of the Passover, held in every Jewish home throughout the world, and the most solemn service of the synagogue on the Day of Atonement, both conclude with the exclamation, 'Next year in Jerusalem.'

The Jewish mind is focused on that magic name *'Yerushalayim,'* which never fails to stir the Jewish heart to the uttermost. An Englishman could perhaps think of England without London, an Irishman of Ireland without Dublin, even a Greek of Greece without Athens, but to the Jews *'Eretz Israel,'* the land of Israel, without Jerusalem is unthinkable."

The Arabs are also opposed to the partition of Palestine. They claim the land is theirs. They want the Jews to remain a minority in a country ruled by a national Arab government. They claim that Great Britain promised the land to them in return for their assistance during the World War. Much has been made of the so-called "McMahon Pledge" when the latter represented British interests in dealing with the Arabs. In a letter to the London Times, Sir Henry McMahon decisively closed the controversy. He wrote: "I feel it my duty to state, and I do so definitely and emphatically, that it was not intended by me in giving this pledge to King Hussein to include Palestine in the area in which Arab independence was promised. I also had every reason to believe at the time that the fact that Palestine was not included in my pledge was well understood by King Hussein."

Not long after the publication of the Royal

JERUSALEM EXTENDING TO THE BROOK KIDRON
Jeremiah predicted that the city would reach the brook of Kidron; this has literally come to pass.

THE "VALLEY OF THE DEAD BODIES"
Jerusalem's boundary line has at last reached this ancient burial place. Some of the cave-like tombs can still be seen.

Commission's report a date was set for a debate on the suggested partition of Palestine in the House of Commons and the House of Lords in London.

In the gracious providence of God, Mrs. Davis and I arrived in London, on our way from Palestine to America, just two days before the time appointed for the debate. We were very eager to be present at the Parliamentary discussion which promisd to be one of historic significance. Friends endeavored to secure for us tickets of admission to the visitors' gallery in the House of Commons. But their efforts were of no avail. At length, as a last resort, a letter of introduction was given us to Sir John Haslam, a consecrated Christian layman, and a member of the House of Commons from Bolton, Lancashire. As we approached the Houses of Parliament we saw people waiting outside the great palace vainly seeking admittance. Armed with the letter of introduction we were allowed to pass one policeman after another, until finally we reached the place where pages take messages to members of Parliament.

It was a day of excitement and the debate was in full swing. We were just feeling that perhaps our quest was in vain, when a fine looking, gray-haired man appeared, with our letter of introduction in his hand. Sir John was most courteous and said he would do the best he could for us. He declared, however, that in all his eleven years in the House of Commons he had never known such a demand for tickets of admission to the visitors' galleries! As we chatted together I found that Sir John had taken an active part in the Torrey-Alexander Mission meetings in Bolton more than 30 years before.

Sir John said he could secure a seat for me in one gallery, and would do his utmost to get one for Mrs. Davis in the ladies' gallery. At length to our delight we found ourselves seated in the galleries of the famous House of Commons! It gave one a thrill to look down at the members of the House and see men whose names have been household words for a generation. In the evening we saw white-haired, but still vigorous, Lloyd George, who as Prime Minister guided the affairs of the British Empire during the World War. Across the aisle from the former Prime Minister sat Winston Churchill, short and rotund, one of the most distinguished statesmen of our generation. I noticed one member wearing a high silk hat. On making inquiry I found he was one of the Rothschild family, famous in finance, who have done so much to help in planting colonies in Palestine.

Never will we forget that memorable and impassioned debate on the partition of Palestine. As soon as one member concluded his address, several persons were on their feet seeking recognition by the Speaker of the House. The debate lasted for fully seven hours. The members of the Government—the party in power—favored the partition plan, the other side opposed it. Mr. Ormsby-Gore, the Colonial Secretary, pleaded for the acceptance of the report of the Royal Commission. He spoke of the "running sore" in Palestine, and said the only cure for it was the division of the country into Arab and Jewish states.

One of the opponents of the Government, Mr. Rothschild, declared the report of the Royal Commission was simply a concession to terrorism. He said it had greatly increased the difficulty of reconciling Jews and Arabs. In impassioned tones he exclaimed: "The Commissioners have torn up the Mandate and the Balfour Declaration! They have gone further. They have torn up Palestine into two or three pieces."

At length Mr. Winston Churchill arose, and pleaded with both sides to avoid making a hasty decision in this momentous matter. He said: "It is a problem about which all the world is looking

FULFILLED IN PALESTINE

to see if Great Britain is going to act in a courageous and sagacious manner."

It was almost midnight when the debate ended. It was decided that later on further discussion should be given to this problem of such far-reaching significance.

Closely following the debate in Parliament came the World Zionist Congress in Zurich. Hundreds of Jewish delegates gathered from many lands, and for days the question of Palestine partition was discussed from all angles. Many of the delegates were opposed to partition in any form.

The President of the Congress was Dr. Chaim Weizmann, the most fascinating and interesting figure in the Jewish world in our day and generation. He was utterly opposed to the boundaries of the partition plan as suggested by the Royal Commission, but was strongly in favor of having the Zionist Executive Committee confer with the British Government on the formation of an independent Jewish state.

In the discussions of the Congress Dr. Weizmann expressed his firm conviction that the formation of a sovereign Jewish state, in fact and not merely in name, would bring great blessing to the Jewish people. He was convinced that with such a state of their own it would be possible to bring 2,000,000 Jews into Palestine during the next 20 or 25 years! He asserted that the Jewish quarters of Jerusalem, with a population of 70,000 Jews, should certainly be included in the Jewish state! He further declared that the Jews must be given the right to build a port wherever necessary, and to control Jewish immigration into the proposed state!

Dr. Ruppin, a great Jewish sociologist, agreed with Dr. Weizmann that the formation of a Jewish state, after these 2000 years, would release enormous Jewish potentialities, and that through such a state, in spite of tremendous difficulties, great things could be achieved in the days to come.

In the course of a two-hour address to the Congress, which was listened to with intense interest, Dr. Weizmann expressed his deep convictions about the present and future of Palestine. He said it was only natural that the Jews should be greatly disappointed over the plans for the partition of Palestine, and over the proposal to set aside such a small area for the Jewish state. He severely criticized the Palestine administration for the lack of firmness they had shown in dealing with the riots of 1936. He said he could not understand why the British army had been relegated to the role of mere spectators of the disorders.

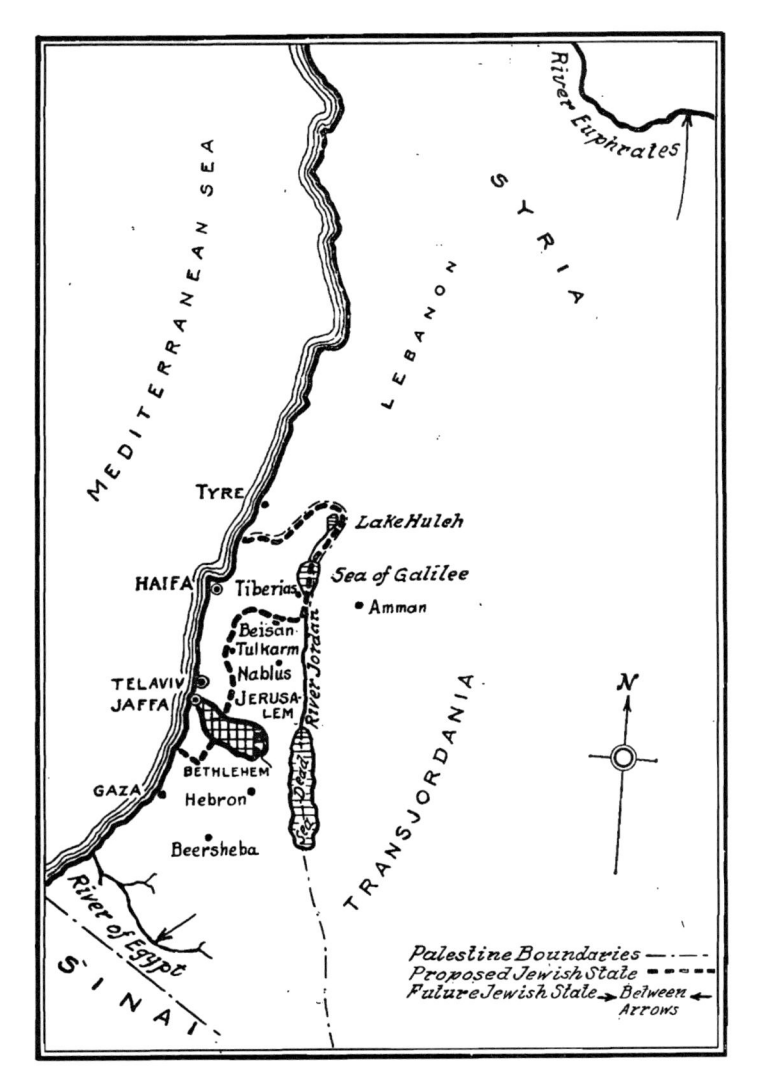

This map shows the small territory set apart for the proposed Jewish state. The arrows indicate the far greater area of the Jewish state of the future.

Dr. Weizmann told the Congress that the real spirit of Great Britain toward the Jews was expressed in the recent parliamentary debate. He said that "no Jew could have noted without emotion the spirit of good will and helpfulness which manifested itself in the debate. It should never be forgotten," he exclaimed, "that the British nation was the only one which, while itself beset by many anxious problems, had made a conscientious effort to find at least a partial solution for the national distress of the Jews!"

Dr. Weizmann stated that he himself was deeply sensitive to the Jewish religion, but he asked the delegates to distinguish between the Messianic hopes and aspirations, and the immediate possibilities. He declared "the Immutable Promise" would come to pass in the fullness of time. The task of the Zionists was to pave the way for the future, and to make the utmost of the opportunities they were now offered.

The most striking and significant thing about the entire question of partition is the prospect that out of all the discussion there may at length emerge an independent Jewish state. If this comes to pass, and it will one way or another in God's time, it will be one of the most remarkable and astonishing events in the modern world—to behold a people that have been wandering in alien

FULFILLED IN PALESTINE 117

countries and under Gentile dominion for nearly 2000 years, once more having their own state and ruler.

During their nineteen centuries of exile the Jews have had no country, no king, no temple, no priest, no sacrifice. This homelessness was accurately pictured by the prophet Hosea more than 2500 years ago. In Hosea, chapter three and verse four, we read: "For the children of Israel shall abide many days without a king, and without a prince, and without a sacrifice."

In the early stages of the proposed new Jewish state the form of government may be democratic. But ere long it will become a monarchy. How do we know this? The Word of God declares it. Just as verse four of this chapter predicted so precisely what has been taking place in the past centuries, so verse five forecasts what will occur in the days to come: "Afterward shall the children of Israel return, and seek the Lord their God, and David their king; and shall fear the Lord and his goodness in the latter days."

When this prophecy was uttered King David had been dead for hundreds of years. This prediction definitely refers to "the latter days." At that time the Jews will look upon King David's greater Son, the Lord Jesus Christ, after His return to the earth in glory and in majesty, and will wholeheartedly accept Him as their Messiah and King. Then in very truth will they "fear the Lord and his goodness in the latter days."

The partition of Palestine may be carried out in our day, but it will not be permanent for it is contrary to God's Word. Palestine will eventually become a Jewish state and its final boundary will be that promised in Genesis 15:18, "From the river of Egypt unto the great river, the river Euphrates." The ruler of the state will be the long promised Messiah, the Lord Jesus Christ.

Chapter X

THE FUTURE OF THE JEWS

It was a June morning in Jerusalem. We were seated, two young men and myself, in the waiting room of a business firm that is playing a prominent part in the rebuilding of Palestine.

While we waited we entered into conversation. I found both young men were Jews. One of them was born in Jerusalem and spoke English and Hebrew fluently. The other had recently come to Palestine from Germany, and his English was rather halting and broken.

As the three of us were alone in the waiting room it seemed to me to be an opporunity to witness for the Lord. I offered one of them a Gospel and the other a New Testament. They received them quite readily, but the young man born in Jerusalem started at once to argue. He declared he was quite all right, was living a good life, and had no sin!

I was beginning to reply to this amazing statement of perfection when the German Jew interrupted us. He wanted to know what my work was, and what had brought me to Palestine. I was very glad to tell them that I was greatly interested in the predictions of the Old Testament prophets about what would happen in Palestine in the latter days. I told them I had come over from America to see how these forecasts made 2500 years ago were being fulfilled today before our very eyes.

They were interested in the statement of my mission in Palestine, but the Jerusalem Jew was still in a mood to argue. Then I told them that I loved the Jews because my Saviour was a Jew. The word "love" acted as a magic wand to open their hearts. The atmosphere of the waiting room suddenly changed. The young man born in Jerusalem lost his desire to argue. Instead he began to tell me of his religious training, and the present state of his soul.

He said he had not been brought up in the orthodox religion of the Jews, and that really he had no belief at all. He felt convinced, however, that people who had beliefs were happier than those who were without them. He had attended churches, and had seen people praying there. He observed that as they went out of the building their faces were very different. They looked as though a stone had been lifted from their souls. He declared he would like to believe, and had tried to believe, but could not do so. And then—

FULFILLED IN PALESTINE

wonder of wonders—he bemoaned the fact that he had so many sins!

What a contrast! Could it be possible that the same young man who a few moments before had contended that he had no sin, was now bewailing the sins that soiled and deadened his soul! The young man's mind was speaking when he said he had no sin; his heart was opening when he confessed his many sins.

I told him how the Old Testament declares that the one thing that will take away our sins is blood: "It is the blood that maketh an atonement for the soul" (Leviticus 17:11). I pointed out to him that the slaying of animals in the Old Testament sacrifices, and the sprinkling of their blood, all looked forward to Christ shedding His blood on the cross of Calvary to make atonement for the sins of all who believe on Him.

By this time both the young men were listening intently. They wanted other questions answered. One of them asked why it was that the Jews had suffered so much and so long. Beginning at Moses I told them of his remarkable predictions, nearly 3500 years ago, of blessings on the people for obedience, and judgments for disobedience. I recounted how these forecasts had been fulfilled to the letter in the history of the Jews.

At length Christ came—a suffering instead of

a reigning Messiah—exactly as predicted by the Old Testament prophets. While many of the Jews received Him as their Messiah and Saviour, yet the leaders of the nation led the populace to reject Him, and to give vent to that awful cry: "His blood be on us, and on our children." Following this self-imposed curse, Moses' prediction of judgments for disobedience came to pass swiftly, and have been of long duration. For nineteen centuries the Jews have been suffering exactly as foretold by their great Lawgiver of long ago.

But today a new thing is taking place before our eyes. Even though the Jewish people as a nation have not acknowledged Jesus as their Messiah, yet God in His great mercy is bringing them back to the land of their forefathers. And further, I told them, the Lord Jesus Christ is soon coming back to Palestine, not this time in lowliness, but in majesty, to rule over Jerusalem, and over all the earth.

At this point the Jerusalem Jew interrupted me with the exclamation: "But, oh, we are so tired of waiting so long for Him to come!"

"Oh," I answered, "He is coming soon. How old are you?"

"Twenty-five," he replied.

"Well," I said, "I may or may not live to wit-

FULFILLED IN PALESTINE

ness His coming, but I feel confident you will live to see Him."

We were still talking of the coming of the Messiah when I was called to see the manager of the firm. He apologized for keeping me waiting for so long a time. But he need not have apologized, for my soul was full of joy that I had been able to witness to two young Jews, who will, quite probably, live to see the return of the Lord in His glory and majesty.

The first coming of Christ was as a Saviour instead of a King. His death and resurrection began the age of grace that has continued for nineteen centuries until the present time. During this period salvation has been not for nations, but for individual believers. In our Lord's remarkable interview with the Jewish ruler Nicodemus, He declared to him that each individual must be born again in order to enter into eternal life. The charter of the age of grace is contained in the statement made by Christ to Nicodemus in John 3: 16: "For God so loved the world, that he gave his only begotten Son, that whosoever believeth in him should not perish, but have everlasting life."

The early Christians were all Jews. On the day of Pentecost, through the preaching of a Jewish follower of Jesus of Nazareth, 3000 Jews accepted Christ as their Saviour in a single day. All through the centuries large numbers of Jews have made the glad discovery that Jesus is the long-promised Messiah, and have put their trust in Him and openly confessed Him as their personal Saviour. It is estimated that during the nineteenth century one Jew in every 156 became a Christian.

It is quite probable that in the present twentieth century an even larger proportion of Jews have found forgiveness of sins and eternal life through faith in the Lord Jesus Christ, and have publicly confessed Him. They have obeyed the words of their Lord in Matthew 10: 32: "Whosoever therefore shall confess me before men, him will I confess also before my Father which is in heaven." They have received the righteousness which is by faith and the joyous assurance of being reconciled to God which comes to those who obey His Word: "That if thou shalt confess with thy mouth the Lord Jesus, and shalt believe in thine heart that God hath raised him from the dead, thou shalt be saved. For with the heart man believeth unto righteousness; and with the mouth confession is made unto salvation" (Romans 10: 9, 10).

There are many Jews who believe in their hearts that Jesus is the Messiah, but they do not have the courage openly to confess Him. In Palestine today many Jews are secret believers. A man there said he could give the names of a hundred Jews in one city in Palestine who believe in Jesus Christ. But they are afraid to declare their faith openly, for to do so would be to lose their means of livelihood. A leading Jew in a synagogue in Palestine said that a number of their members believe that Jesus is the Messiah, but they are not willing that others should know of their belief.

Today there is a readiness among the Jews throughout the world to read the Bible, and to listen to the Gospel message, an openmindedness that was utterly lacking a generation ago. I was recently conversing with a well known Bible teacher who has labored in home and foreign lands. He made this striking statement: "I believe the Jews throughout the world today are more ready to receive the Word of God than at any time since the day of Pentecost."

But as a nation the Jews are still in unbelief and will remain so until the coming of the Messiah. Because the Jews as a nation rejected Christ as their Saviour, they were scattered to the ends of the earth. Today, however, they are being regathered though still with the veil of unbelief over their eyes. Why are they being called back to their own land? First, because it is "the set time," appointed from all eternity, for their return. Second, because large numbers must be in the land to receive the Messiah with open hearts and arms when He appears in glory. The prophecy of Jeremiah in chapter 31, verse 10, is having a preliminary fulfillment today before our eyes: "Hear the word of the Lord, O ye nations, and declare it in the isles afar off, and say, He that scattered Israel will gather him, and keep him, as a shepherd doth his flock."

But the return of the Jews to Palestine will by no manner of means mark the end of their troubles. The "time of Jacob's trouble" is still future. The present disturbances in Palestine are a small thing compared to the tribulation they are yet to endure. But deliverance will come to them. The prophet Jeremiah pictures the event in chapter 30, verse 7: "Alas! for that day is great, so that none is like it: it is even the time of Jacob's trouble, but he shall be saved out of it."

As the Jews return to Palestine in larger and larger numbers, the land will be increasingly fruitful and prosperous. In a previous book, "Rebuilding Palestine According to Prophecy," we told how the potential value of the mineral salts in the Dead Sea water is estimated at one trillion, two hundred and seventy billion dollars—

HAIFA AND ITS HARBOR
Haifa is on the shore of the Mediterranean Sea and extends up the slopes of Mount Carmel.

BUILDING IN HAIFA HARBOR DISTRICT
Haifa is still growing rapidly. Its population has nearly or quite reached the one hundred thousand mark.

or about as much as the combined wealth of the rest of the world!

A number of nations, lured on by their lust for the wealth of the land of Palestine, with its strategic position, will combine their forces, and march against it. The prophet Ezekiel, writing more than 2500 years ago, addresses the enemies that are filled with greed to possess the land: "In the latter years thou shalt come into the land that is brought back from the sword, and is gathered out of many people, against the mountains of Israel, which have been always waste: but it is brought forth out of the nations, and they shall dwell safely all of them. . . . And thou shalt say, I will go up . . . to take a spoil, and to take a prey; to turn thine hand upon the desolate places that are now inhabited, and upon the people that are gathered out of the nations, which have gotten cattle and goods, that dwell in the midst of the land" (Ezekiel 38: 8, 11a, 12).

Listen to Ezekiel's description of the onward march of the enemies of the Jews to overwhelm the land of Palestine: "Thou shalt ascend and come like a storm, thou shalt be like a cloud to cover the land, thou, and all thy bands, and many people with thee" (Ezekiel 38:9).

When it seems as if the Jews are about to be annihilated by their enemies, they will cry to God in agony of soul to save them from destruction. God will answer their cry and give divine deliverance. There will be a mighty earthquake. Their Messiah will suddenly descend from heaven and smite and utterly destroy their enemies (Ezekiel 38:18-22). It will be a victory and deliverance greater than any of those recorded in the history of the Jews from their beginning as a nation.

The Lord Himself, speaking through the prophet Ezekiel, describes the effect of the supernatural victory upon the nations throughout the world: "Thus will I magnify myself, and sanctify myself; and I will be known in the eyes of many nations, and they shall know that I am the Lord" (Ezekiel 38: 23).

But the most amazed of all people will be the Jews themselves. They will be astonished not only at the great victory, but at the Victor Himself. As they behold Him they will see that their Deliverer is nail-pierced! Lo, their Messiah is none other than the Lord Jesus Christ whom the nation had been rejecting for nineteen long centuries! The prophet Zechariah vividly portrays their repentance and poignant sorrow as they make this discovery: "And I will pour upon the house of David, and upon the inhabitants of Jerusalem, the spirit of grace and of supplications: and they shall look upon me whom they have pierced, and they shall mourn for him, as one mourneth for his only son, and shall be in bitterness for him, as one that is in bitterness for his firstborn. . . . In that day there shall be a fountain opened to the house of David and to the inhabitants of Jerusalem for sin and for uncleanness" (Zechariah 12:10; 13:1).

"There is a fountain filled with blood,
  Drawn from Immanuel's veins;
  And sinners, plunged beneath that flood,
  Lose all their guilty stains."

The news of the Messiah's appearance and victory will bring unbounded joy to Jews throughout the world. In every land they will vie with one another to get back to their homeland with all speed. Palestine will be utterly inadequate to contain the returning millions. But their territory, under the rule of David's greater Son, will extend, as it did long ago under King Solomon, "from the river of Egypt unto the great river, the river Euphrates." That land that is now waste and desolate will then blossom as the rose, and be like a watered garden.

In glowing language the Old Testament prophets picture the blessing and the glory of those great and happy days under the rule and reign of the Messiah. Isaiah gives a graphic description of the Jews hurrying back to their country and their King. They will sell their possessions and take their wealth back with them. Some will be in such haste to get to Palestine that they will go by airplane. Others, with more baggage to carry, will be compelled to travel by the slower method of steamships. Isaiah forecasts the scene in chapter 60, verses 8 and 9: "Who are these that fly as a cloud, and as the doves to their windows? Surely the isles shall wait for me, and the ships of Tarshish first, to bring thy sons from far, their silver and their gold with them, unto the name of the Lord thy God, and to the Holy One of Israel, because He hath glorified thee."

The Jews will then be God's heralds to bring untold blessing to the other nations of the earth. They will go forth to tell the people of all lands of the greatness and glory of the Messiah, the Son of God.

The coming of Messiah will usher in the golden age of a thousand years of righteousness, under the rule of David's greater Son, the Lord Jesus Christ. The Devil will be chained. War will be abolished. Universal peace, the dream of the ages, will at last come to pass through the reign of the Prince of Peace.

In those days there will be no anti-Semitism in Germany or Poland, or in any other land. The

Jews will be the most favored and fortunate people in the world. They will be—as they always have been—the blood relations of the once rejected, but then accepted and adored Messiah. The people that have been so long despised will be the most honored and esteemed of all the inhabitants of the earth. Isaiah tells how those that once afflicted them will then bow down to them: "The sons also of them that afflicted thee shall come bending unto thee; and all they that despised thee shall bow themselves down at the soles of thy feet; and they shall call thee, The city of the Lord, The Zion of the Holy One of Israel" (Isaiah 60:14).

In that golden era there will be no more rioting in the land of Palestine. The days of violence and destruction will be ended, and the age of peace and concord will be established: "Violence shall no more be heard in thy land, wasting nor destruction within thy borders; but thou shalt call thy walls Salvation, and thy gates Praise.... For the Lord shall be thine everlasting light, and the days of thy mourning shall be ended. Thy people also shall be all righteous: they shall inherit the land for ever, the branch of my planting, the work of my hands, that I may be glorified" (Isaiah 60:18, 20, 21).

EPILOGUE

SHOWING OTHERS THE WONDROUS WORKS OF GOD

The fulfillment of Old Testament predictions, uttered 2500 years ago, proves beyond any peradventure of doubt the truthfulness and divine inspiration of the Word of God. The record of these facts is a tonic to faith in these days of doubt and unbelief.

God is working wondrously in Palestine today, and surely He wants people—believers and unbelievers alike—to know what He is doing. This book tells something of His work, and of fulfilled prophecies that prove the supernatural inspiration of the Bible.

You can have a share in letting people know how God is working, and how prophecy is being fulfilled, by giving copies of this book to others.

You might do a real work for God by sending for a supply of the book, and giving copies to relatives and friends and to Christian workers and leaders in your church. Much good might also result from your giving the book to Jews in your community as they are greatly interested in anything relating to Palestine.

Special rates have been made to aid in the widespread distribution of the book. One copy, postpaid, 25 cents; five copies, postpaid to one address, $1.00; 12 copies, postpaid to the same address, $2.25; 25 copies, postpaid to the same address, $4.50. In larger quantities 50 copies will be sent for $8.00, express charges collect; 100 copies for $15.00, express charges collect. When single copies are sent *to different addresses,* it is necessary to charge 25 cents each.

The above prices are for the books bound in paper covers. In cloth binding the price of the book is 50 cents each, or 5 copies for $2.25.

It would surely bring great blessing to your church or Sunday school or Bible class or mission to have 25 or 50 or 100 copies of this book given to officers and teachers and leading members to quicken their faith in the Bible, and to stimulate their interest in the return of the Lord.

Long ago King David said: "That I may publish with the voice of thanksgiving, and tell of all thy wondrous works." So it is a privilege to show others God's wondrous works in Palestine; that the Bible is the inspired Word of God; and that the return of the Lord is near at hand.